Wings of Destiny

The Story of

Fifth Angel

BRIAN J. HEATON

Wings of Destiny: The Story of Fifth Angel

Copyright © 2025, Breakdown Room Publishing, LLC.

All rights reserved.

No part of this book can be reproduced or transmitted in any form, or by any means electronic or mechanical, including photography, recording, or any information storage and retrieval system, without written permission from the author and copyright holder.

Cover art and book design by Cyrusfiction Productions.
Cover concept by Brian J. Heaton.

Edited by Brian J. Heaton.
First published in Fall 2025.

All images are the property of the author except where otherwise noted.

ISBN: 979-8-9918449-2-5 (Paperback)
ISBN: 979-8-9918449-3-2 (Hardcover)

www.breakdownroom.net

Contents

Foreword, by Ed Archer	IV
Introduction	VI
Chapter 1: Genesis	1
At the Precipice: 1979 Battle of the Bands	28
Chapter 2: Call Out the Warning	33
In His Words: James Byrd	55
From the Congregation: Brian L. Naron	59
Chapter 3: Making the Climb	63
In His Words: Ed Archer	85
Chapter 4: Only the Strong Survive	89
In His Words: John Macko	102
Chapter 5: Time Will Tell	105
Video Shoot Itinerary	131
Chapter 6: Into Waiting Darkness	137
In His Words: Ed Archer	152
Chapter 7: Resurrection	155
Chapter 8: Day Into Night	171
Chapter 9: We Will Rise	193
From the Congregation: James R. Beach	213
Chapter 10: Angels of Mercy	215
From the Congregation: Mike Gaube	233
Chapter 11: Light the Skies	237
Epilogue	258
Acknowledgements	261
Author Interviews	264
Works Cited	265
Fifth Angel Concert History	268
Author Bio	270

Foreword

When Brian first told me he was considering writing a biography about Fifth Angel, I thought, "Wow, Brian is the perfect fit to write such a book!"

After all, Brian was a diehard fan from the start, way back when he was barely a teenager and we were twenty-something heavy metal wannabes, with our first album coming out. And years later, Brian faithfully created a website to honor the band, back when the internet was still "new" and the band had been disbanded for years. That's when I first became aware of who Brian was, and we quickly became good friends. When Fifth Angel decided to become active again in 2009, Brian was there, helping us navigate our "second coming." So, who else to write such a definitive book? Nobody but Brian!

This book tells a story that is probably not all that unusual for a lot of bands—how a band forms, develops, and evolves musically to find "their sound." But Fifth Angel's story is also unique. Our blend of personalities, the events that unfolded, the state of the music industry at the time, and the band's geographic location certainly helped carve a distinctive path for Fifth Angel, particularly during our first era. Yes indeed, there are a lot of different factors and variables for any band during its infancy, and beyond!

Fast forward to more recent years, the unexpected interest and resurgence of "legacy metal" from the 1980s took us off-guard, but the timing was perfect! The new incarnation of Fifth Angel was ready and willing to serve, with festival invites coming in from different parts of the world and an unexpected offer to record new music. This gave an opportunity for different band members to introduce their musical offerings, but most importantly, for old (and new) fans to come hear us play live! This has been especially meaningful, considering that Fifth Angel never toured or played live during its original tenure in the 1980s. It is humbling to know that the music we worked so hard on so many years ago is still appreciated!

I hope you enjoy the book. Happy reading to you!

Ed Archer, Fifth Angel
June 2025

Ed Archer and Brian Heaton on April 22, 2017, at El Corazón, in Seattle, Washington.

Introduction

My rock and roll journey started in the mid-1980s with Survivor's *Vital Signs*, Bon Jovi's *Slippery When Wet*, and Whitesnake's self-titled album. I was hooked on the big choruses, catchy guitar solos, and bluesy riffs that I heard on those records. But everything changed for me on a chilly winter afternoon in early 1988.

My friends Jeff and Wayne Douglass popped a dubbed cassette copy of Fifth Angel's self-titled debut into the boombox in their shared bedroom where we were hanging out. Immediately, all three of us knew it was something incredibly different and special. The music was heavier than we had heard before up to that point, and the lyrics weren't about girls and partying. Fifth Angel took a different route with their songs, writing about the threat of global nuclear war, and broader social and theological issues. I don't think we understood a lot of that back then, but "In the Fallout," "The Night," "Fade to Flames," etc., all just resonated with us. Fifth Angel had something to say, and we were listening.

I was obsessed with the album then, and I still am today. *Fifth Angel* remains one of my all-time favorite recordings by any band. It was a watershed moment in my life when I first heard it, with the album serving as a bedrock for the type of music I still love today—thought-provoking heavy metal and hard rock.

I acquired my own dubbed cassette of *Fifth Angel* from my friends and played it until the tape warped. I spent countless hours going to music stores, hoping to find a legitimate replacement. After many unsuccessful attempts at acquiring my "Holy Grail," I found *Fifth Angel* at Tape World, a record store chain with a location inside the Smith Haven Mall in

Lake Grove, Long Island, New York. In fact, I found two copies. The original version, released on Shrapnel Records in 1986, and the 1988 reissue by Epic Records. Being a young music fan, I wasn't sure what the difference was (remember, this was before the internet, and I was 12 years old), but I noticed they contained the same songs and so I bought the former because of the more striking album cover. (And later, I'd buy the reissue, too.)

By 1989, I was pining for a new Fifth Angel album. I saw a few small articles that praised them in various rock and metal magazines, but mentions of the band were scarce. About six months later, I came across a promotional advertisement for a new Fifth Angel record called *Time Will Tell*. I was ecstatic. There was just one problem. The ad didn't show the album's release date and none of the local record shops had any idea who Fifth Angel was, nor when *Time Will Tell* was due to hit the shelves. That seemed odd to me, but I held out hope. I begged my mother that if I could only have one thing for Christmas that year, I'd love it if my present could be Fifth Angel's *Time Will Tell* on cassette.

"Santa" Mom delivered. *Time Will Tell* was in my Christmas stocking in the wee hours of December 25, 1989. I must have played it two or three times before falling back to sleep. I remember being enamored right away with "Cathedral," "Seven Hours," and "We Rule" in particular, as those reminded me of the lyrical concepts from the first album. I slept fitfully for a few hours after that, until Christmas morning began in earnest. The voice of Ted Pilot and the heavy riffs still hit home for me. It felt like a reunion with good friends, a feeling that would be ironic many years later.

I wrote a letter to Fifth Angel in spring 1990, and distinctly recall being so excited to send it, hoping for a response. Sadly, that answer never came. I don't remember how I found out, but I learned Fifth Angel broke up, likely a few weeks after I sent them the letter. I was gutted that the band was no longer together.

And in a cruel twist of fate, Fifth Angel's split happened before the band received some notoriety with "Midnight Love" from *Time Will Tell* serving as the opening theme of *The Howard Stern Show* in summer 1990. Despite their disbandment, I continued to be a hardcore fan of Fifth Angel's music. The group's two albums were in my regular listening rotation for years to come.

A decade later, I saw that James Byrd, the lead guitarist on Fifth Angel's first album, had a website. I reached out to Byrd via email, telling him that I was a massive fan and gushed about the record. To my surprise, Byrd graciously replied, taking my exuberance in stride. We struck up a good conversation and eventually, a casual friendship, and he explained his perspective on why he and Fifth Angel parted ways and some of the frustrations he had with his former bandmates. A few more years passed, and James was gracious enough to invite my wife and me to his home for coffee in November 2006. He surprised us with a special guest, the man who took his place as lead guitarist in Fifth Angel, Kendall Bechtel. It was a great afternoon of conversation.

Around the same time, after finally acquiring both Fifth Angel albums on vinyl (I had multiple copies on cassette and CD by that point), I was able to look up and contact all the band members and ask if they would autograph the LP covers and mail them back to me. They all kindly agreed, saying how thankful they were that their music was still appreciated. Since no website for Fifth Angel existed at that time, I took it upon myself to create one in 2006-2007. For several years, it stood as the only online information hub for the band.

Moving forward, I was privileged to have contact with the band members from time to time, adding content to the website and interviewing them for articles. In 2009, Ed Archer reached out. Along with bassist John Macko, and lead guitarist Kendall Bechtel, the trio were reuniting Fifth Angel with some new members, including drummer Jeffrey McCormack, for the Keep it True (KIT) festival in Germany the following year. Ed invited me to visit and attend the band's rehearsals.

I flew up to Seattle in April 2010. Myself and two local friends, Jonathan Rustvold and Jeff Brown, watched Fifth Angel play their entire set (without vocals) in Ed's basement. I positioned myself in front of Kendall's monitor and proceeded to sing every song at the top of my lungs for an hour. Kendall noticed I knew all the words and could sing. After a quick break, they motioned me up to the front, and I sang "The Night," "We Rule," and Fifth Angel's version of the UFO classic "Lights Out" with the band.

Unfortunately, by then my voice was shot from singing over the extremely high volume (which to this day, I regret). But the experience was a "pinch me" moment I'll never forget, and I was eternally grateful for the opportunity to live out one of my childhood dreams of fronting the mighty Fifth Angel. Hey, it was a fun 15 minutes of fame!

About a week later, Fifth Angel made its live debut at Keep it True with fill-in singer Peter Orullian. They received a raucous ovation from the metal-loving German audience. The band asked me to manage them, which I did for a brief time as they demoed new music. I stepped down a few months later, however, as I found I couldn't separate my growing friendship with some of the members from the work I needed to do as Fifth Angel's manager.

After some lineup changes, Fifth Angel continues to soar today—over 40 years since they first got together. And I'm still riding on the wings, proud to tell their captivating story.

James Byrd, Brian Heaton, and Kendall Bechtel on October 14, 2006.

Brian Heaton, Ed Archer, John Macko, and Kendall Bechtel in April 2010, at the Hard Rock Café, in Seattle, Washington.

Author Brian Heaton poses with Kendall Bechtel, John Macko, Jeffrey McCormack, and Ted Pilot after Fifth Angel's performance on April 22, 2017.

> "Fifth Angel could turn out to be something of a real gem, sparkling all the way along the road to an outpocket called greatness."
>
> – Malcolm Dome, *Kerrang!*

Chapter 1
Genesis

When thinking about Seattle's place in music history, the term "grunge" should instinctively come to mind. Pacific Northwest bands such as Alice in Chains, Nirvana, Pearl Jam, and Soundgarden served as the poster children for heavy alternative rock in the 1990s. They epitomized raw power and emotion, and appealed to followers of punk, hardcore, and heavy metal.

From a mainstream perspective, the "core four" of grunge in Seattle were highly influenced by acts of the 1960s and 1970s, such as Black Sabbath, Led Zeppelin, the Ramones, the Sex Pistols, and Seattle's own Jimi Hendrix and Heart. Grunge and the rise of the internet put the region's music scene on the map for a new generation of listeners. But before the Emerald City became synonymous with the Rooster, teen spirit, a kid named Jeremy, and looking California and feeling Minnesota, the area was home to some of the world's most unique and powerful hard rock and heavy metal bands.

One of the most influential groups was TKO, which was formed in the late 1970s. TKO was led by singer Brad Sinsel and guitarist Rick Pierce. They were signed by Infinity Records, a division of MCA Records, and released *Let it Roll* in 1979. TKO toured with the likes of Van Halen, Cheap Trick, and AC/DC, and the album sold over 150,000 copies.

Unfortunately, Infinity Records folded, was absorbed by MCA, and TKO didn't get another record deal until several years later.

Rail was another example of success for many aspiring rock musicians in Seattle. The group formed in 1970, under the name "Rail & Company," and slugged it out in the clubs for years, playing hundreds of shows (along with shortening their name). They played cover tunes and a few originals, working hard to make it. Eventually, Rail landed a support slot on Van Halen's 1980 tour in support of *Women and Children First*. But it took a decade for Rail to score a record deal and release their first album, *Arrival*.

"Rail should have made it; they're tremendous musicians," said guitarist James Byrd. "But they overexposed themselves in the Northwest. They burned themselves out."

But the early success of both TKO and Rail lit the match and inspired other groups to carry the torch and make their mark. Culprit and Metal Church (first known as "Shrapnel") rose up, got signed, and put out records. One of the most successful torchbearers was Queensrÿche (initially called "The Mob"), hailing from Bellevue, Washington.

Unlike many of the local acts at the time, Queensrÿche didn't play the clubs. Other than a handful of early local shows they performed as "The Mob," which was strictly a cover band, the musicians of Queensrÿche instead honed their original songs, and self-financed and recorded an EP on their own independent label, 206 Records. Thanks to managers Kim and Diana Harris, who dropped a copy of the EP at various rock music publications in London while on vacation, Queensrÿche's EP got a glowing review in *Kerrang!* which set off a firestorm of interest in the band. Ultimately, after seeing the band perform at a private rehearsal, EMI Records signed Queensrÿche to a seven-album deal,[1] which eventually led the group to stardom.

As is wont to happen, major labels started scouring the Seattle area to find the "next" Queensrÿche. Eventually, Metal Church was picked up by Elektra Records in 1985, and hotshot guitarist Adam Bomb (Adam Brenner) signed with Geffen Records. But Queensrÿche's method of working on their original material and not playing shows had proved fruitful, and several of their local peers took notice.

One of the musicians paying attention to Queensrÿche's success was a guitarist named James Byrd. Born on July 23, in the early 1960s, to Paul and Jean Herbold, James was raised in Bellingham, Washington, just north of Seattle. Byrd received his first guitar at age two. It was a Mickey Mouse guitar, just a toy, really. Byrd's sister, however, got a real guitar, and when she wouldn't let him play it, he forgot about the instrument until he was about eight years old. Byrd was taking piano lessons then, but wanted to play guitar, and his mother relented and purchased young James a smaller, student-sized guitar, for around $12.

But Byrd didn't get serious about playing guitar until tragedy stuck—the death of Jimi Hendrix on September 18, 1970. After watching a news clip of Hendrix performing the United States National Anthem at Woodstock, Byrd found his calling. His parents refused to buy him an electric guitar, but James persevered, saving every dime he earned from doing chores. After some time, he bought a cheap electric guitar and amp and began studying some of the masters of classical music and blues-based rock.

---

1. Learn more about Queensrÿche in *Roads to Madness: The Touring History of Queensrÿche (1981-1997)* and *Building an Empire: The Story of Queensrÿche*.

Some of Byrd's early influences include Hendrix, B.B. King, and Johnny Winter. As he got older, James became an expert blues guitarist, and started listening to other types of players who helped shape his sound. Ritchie Blackmore, Uli Jon Roth, Frank Marino, Al Di Meola, Neal Schon and Michael Schenker all left an impact on young Byrd, who put together his first band, Wizard, at age 12.

"It lasted long enough to practice outside in the backyard and draw a crowd and the attention of the police," Byrd said of Wizard.

Wizard went on to play one school dance and quickly called it a day. But Byrd was undaunted, lying about his age so he could take gigs playing with bands in bars. Eventually, Byrd's obsession with the guitar turned into an aspiration to make his living playing music. Once he was 18, Byrd hit the road in a heavy metal cover band called Hard Luck, based out of Wenatchee, Washington. Hard Luck provided Byrd with valuable stage experience, as the group performed all over the Northwest, with a setlist comprised of songs by UFO and the Scorpions. Hard Luck had some notoriety, winning a "Battle of the Bands" competition, which earned the group free studio time. With no original songs, the band simply recorded many of the cover songs they had been playing on the road.

Playing music from other bands wasn't enough for Byrd, however. In 1980, he moved to Seattle and started working on original songs. He had a band called To Excess, and Byrd played shows with them around Seattle. But it wasn't long before the guitarist set his sights on the Los Angeles rock scene.

"I had joined another band when I first came to Seattle, and I went on the road with them," Byrd said. "Interestingly enough, they were a band with a full horn section. They were actually based out of Las Vegas. A high production value show band.

They filed for bankruptcy shortly after I joined them and broke up. But I followed the vocalist and one other band member to LA—they invited me to come with them. I ended up going there with a brown paper bag and a guitar and sleeping on a sofa. So that's how I got to LA. [I did] all the usual shit down there. Played all the usual places, The Troubadour, Perkins Palace."

By late-1982, Byrd had tired of Los Angeles and moved back to Seattle to pursue a new, heavier musical direction. He hoped to work with a singer who was making a name for himself in the area—Ted Pilot.

Ted Pilot was born in April 1961, in Seattle, Washington. He started playing guitar and piano when he was about 12 years old. As young musicians do, Pilot and some friends started a band in junior high school, and he ended up playing lead guitar for a while. At some point, the singer of that band threw a fit, which provided an opportunity for Pilot to expand his musical abilities.

"Our singer at the time, I can't remember his name because we were just kids, he was a little bit of a prima donna," Pilot said. "One day, he got mad at us and quit. We just went around the room and saw who could sing the best. That's how I got started as a singer. It came to my turn, and people went, 'Wow, you can really sing.' So, I became the lead guitar player and vocalist."

Pilot's mother was very supportive of her son's musical endeavors. As for his father, who was a dentist, Ted said he "tolerated" his son's music and let them rehearse in the house thinking it was just a phase. The singer remembered his dad always saying that having the band at his house was better than "going out and raising hell somewhere else."

Sadly, Ted's mother passed away from metastatic breast cancer in 1978. Dr. Pilot raised Ted, along with his brother and sister, from that point forward. It was around then when music became a bigger priority for Ted, and the singer started taking the cover band a bit more seriously.

Pilot was very enamored with singers who had distinctive voices, such as Ronnie James Dio, Robert Plant, and Mick Jagger. Pilot wanted to find his own voice and eventually started taking vocal lessons from esteemed instructor David Kyle,[2] who taught the young singer what he needed to know about diaphragm support and good technique.

"What I think makes a vocalist really good, besides the basics of pitch control and vocal support and stuff like that, is the uniqueness of their voice," Pilot said. "That's one of the things I always strove for is, if you heard me sing, it's a unique voice, it sounds like me."

Like Pilot, Edward Sein was born in April 1961, in Seattle, Washington. His parents were Vic and Sue Sein. Ed's mother was a good singer and piano player who listened to the radio often. Ed would hear the music and try to pick out the melody on the piano that his family had in the house. Sue's sister was visiting one day and pointed out that Ed had an inclination toward music, and Sue signed her son up for a rhythm class that introduced young children to instruments such as the xylophone, triangle and maracas. Ed was about age four or five at the time.

As Ed grew older, he started playing violin and took formal

---

2. Maestro David Paul Kyle was an iconic voice instructor in Seattle. He taught singers such as Ann Wilson (Heart), Geoff Tate (Queensrÿche), Layne Staley (Alice in Chains), and Chris Cornell (Soundgarden). He passed away on November 27, 2004.

lessons on the piano. By age eight, Ed switched from the violin to the cello. He became very involved in his school's orchestra program. Eventually, Ed got more advanced in reading music and his abilities expanded as he got into his teenage years. But once he discovered rock music, his life changed immediately.

"That was probably because of some neighborhood kids who were listening to the local rock station, which back in those days was an AM radio station, WKJR," Sein recalled. "This DJ, who went by 'Emperor Smith,' played The Doors and Jethro Tull and I kept hearing guitar on these songs, and that's what drew me in."

Ed asked for and received an electric guitar for Christmas. Vic Sein had a copy of the *Layfette Radio Electronics* catalog, and the guitar and small amplifier Ed received was ordered from that. Ed started taking guitar lessons and quickly discovered a love for the instrument.

The burgeoning musician remembered having an easier time learning the guitar due to his exposure to violin and cello. Ed's guitar skills improved quickly. His first guitar teacher, Jeff Freewalt, was more of a jazz and blues player and passed techniques in those styles down to Ed. In fact, Ed still has all the handwritten lessons that Freewalt taught him.

By the end of sixth grade, Ed gave up the cello and proceeded full steam ahead with guitar. But he was confused as to why what he was playing didn't sound like what he heard on the radio. Freewalt told him about distortion, and a lightbulb went off for Ed. He picked up the EHX Big Muff Pi fuzz pedal. It helped, but it wasn't the true distorted sound Ed was seeking. He then went down the rabbit hole, learning about the differences between transistor and tube distortion, different types of pedals and guitar pickups.

FM radio started getting popular and this only fed Ed's fervor for guitar. Now in junior high school, Ed was listening to

Pink Floyd and Led Zeppelin. Jimmy Page was a huge influence on Ed's playing, and still is.

"Hearing Led Zeppelin was a pivotal moment for me. It really drew me in, especially with Jimmy Page, and his songwriting," Sein said. "Then there was Black Sabbath, and when I heard 'Iron Man' on the radio, that really piqued my interest. I remember learning that and then going out and getting a Black Sabbath record. But then I heard Deep Purple and *Machine Head*—wow, man, to this day when I listen to that record from the first song on side one to the last song on side two, the energy is just amazing."

Eventually, Ed took his playing to the next level, joining a garage band with some friends from school. Although the fledging group never performed publicly, Ed remembers them setting up in his backyard with another guitar player and a friend of his that was a drummer. They just jammed for an afternoon, typical teenagers playing tunes that they all liked. Eventually, everyone went their separate ways. Once he got into Newport High School, in Bellevue, Washington, however, Ed's playing got much more serious.

In 1976, Ed remembered drawing stacks of amplifiers in his notebook during a speech class, which was noticed by a classmate, Greg Keeney. Keeney was a bass player and mentioned to Ed that he had another friend who played guitar. That friend's name was Ted Pilot.

"I remember meeting Ted during lunchtime, and it was very casual, nothing Earth-shattering. But later, we talked about jamming," Sein said. "We got together, Ted and I were both playing guitar with Greg on bass, and Ted was singing, and it sounded pretty decent. Fast-forward a couple of months, and at this point we were pretty good at being able to learn a song and play it in unison. We started developing a cover song set list, but we didn't have a drummer."

Ken Mary was born in September, and grew up in Seattle, Washington, during the late-1960s and 1970s. From age five, he knew his future was in music. Teachers took away pencils and pens because he was pounding on desks and different objects all the time. Despite his "practice" being distracting to teachers and his fellow students, Ken's excitement for music was encouraged by his mother, and his talent flourished.

"I didn't grow up in a rich family; for my mother to sacrifice and buy me a kit of drums was a big deal," Mary said. "I really admire that about my mother; that she tried to support our dreams and whatever. She saw that drums were something I had a passion for, and she supported it."

Ken's ability on the drums was quickly noticed by friends in school. He initially learned to play with traditional grip, listening to jazz, Latin, and fusion players. He moved to using a matched grip when he started playing rock, citing Steve Gadd, Tommy Aldridge, Neil Peart, and Dave Weckl as influences. But his biggest musical hero was Buddy Rich.

"Although as a person he certainly had his challenges, he was considered in his day, and still today, as perhaps the greatest drummer ever," Mary said of Rich. "I agree that is true, based on the fact that 30 years after his death, videos of his solos are still astounding drummers. Stylistically, he had something amazing as well; I just don't get bored watching him, and there is fire coming off of those drumsticks."

It wasn't long before Ken was in junior high school and started playing professional gigs throughout the Pacific Northwest.

Pilot, Archer and Keeney rapidly developed as a band. Called "Ridge," the group got together to play a few songs by Cheap Trick, Ted Nugent, Van Halen, and others, and discovered they had good chemistry and started rehearsing regularly.

"Ted was a real hoot to hang out with," Sein recalled. "Very witty, very funny and very smart. And of course, having the gift of being very musical. Being in a new school and meeting new people, as they say, 'birds of a feather flock together' and Ted was a part of my new 'musical friend group.'"

With a stable of songs to play, Ridge now needed a drummer to start gigging. A friend of the group, Scott Davidson, suggested Ken Mary, who was barely in junior high school at the time. But Davidson praised Mary's skill, and Ridge auditioned him. It was quickly obvious that Ken was the guy for the job.

"He was really good, even at that young age," Sein said. "Amazingly good, amazingly talented. And that was the beginning, the start of Ridge."

"I was always the youngest guy in every band I've ever been in," Mary added. "They came to see me at a talent show at my junior high. I was a skilled player. My talent always pushed me into a different league. My age never really was an issue."

Ridge started learning how to play more of the rock radio hits of the day that they heard on KZOK and KISW out of Seattle. They initially focused on a balance of danceable tunes and some heavier cuts such as "2112" by Rush and "Beyond the Realms of Death" by Judas Priest. That balance served Ridge well, as the group quickly picked up a legion of devoted fans, including a large female following.

"What was kind of funny was that some of the music that in our mind we thought wasn't very danceable, we would get in and play it and people would find a way to dance to it anyway," Sein said.

Ridge's first public appearance was at the 7th Annual Newport Follies Variety Show at Newport Senior High School, in Bellevue. The gig, which was a talent show, took place on April 20-21, 1978. Ridge took home first place, garnering 203 votes.[3]

By the time 1979 rolled around, Ridge was being booked by Craig Cooke and Jim Smith of UniCam Entertainment. They played gigs all over Washington, from Bellevue and Seattle to Port Townsend, Port Angeles, and Spokane. Ridge was successful, selling T-shirts in droves, partying, and building a reputation as a tight live band.

In summer 1979, Ridge entered a 16-band Battle of the Bands held at the Crossroads Lake Hills Roller Rink in Bellevue, Washington. The competition lasted for six weeks, with bands playing each week until the final concert on Tuesday, August 28, 1979. Ridge emerged victorious over the band Tyrant, which boosted Ridge's profile. But change was afoot, as Keeney decided to leave the band. Ironically, he was replaced by Tyrant bassist Randy Nelson.

Ridge played hundreds of shows over the span of just a few years, mostly on weekends when the guys weren't in school or working. It was also a family affair, as Ted's brother, Matt Pilot, helped the band out at many of the shows. One of Ridge's favorite venues was Mr. Bill's in the Northgate neighborhood of Seattle. The all-ages club was located at 832 NE Northgate Way[4] and the band regularly pulled in about 500 people each time they played.

---

3. The variety show's MC was Jeff Probst. Probst later won an Emmy Award as host of the reality show *Survivor*.

4. The location where Mr. Bill's stood is now a Rockler Woodworking & Hardware store (as of April 2025).

"Mr. Bill's was a cool place, but it eventually got to be too over the top," Sein said. "I remember when the police started patrolling from the roof so they could look down on the crowd in the parking lot and radio down to a unit down below. [There was] much partying in the parking lot; I'm sure the neighborhood residents didn't appreciate it."

Aspiring guitarist, and later vocalist, Tim Branom, was one of Ridge's big fans. He remembered going to their shows and being enamored with the group's sound.

"I thought Ridge were great, and I would go out and see them, and somehow I struck up a friendship with the bass player Randy Nelson," Branom said. "Then I was in Bandstand Music in Bellevue, and I saw a sign that said, 'Ridge looking for a second guitar player.' I was only 16 years old, or a little bit older, I guess. But I went down and jammed with the guys, and it was fun, but while I was good, I wasn't good enough. I was a little too young."

According to Ted Pilot, some of Ridge's notable gigs included performing at the Paramount Theatre in Seattle twice (December 1979 and again in 1980), and the Moore Theatre.

By 1982, however, Ridge was tired of playing music from other bands. They wanted to write their own songs and went in the studio to cut a few tracks. One of them was called "Screaming with Delight," which Ridge played in their set in addition to the cover songs. But the experiment was short-lived. The members could not agree on a focused musical direction, and eventually, Ridge broke up.

"We had a lot of jobs in taverns, the typical thing that bands do, playing for taverns, playing in small halls, like everybody else tries to do," Pilot said. "Finally, one day, we decided it was time for a change. The band basically split up, and we went our separate ways."

Eventually, Pilot and Sein linked up with guitarist Mark von Beck, and along with Nelson on bass, and Greg Thompson on drums,[5] formed Glass. Glass featured more of a "jangly" guitar sound with von Beck's new wave influences bringing a semi-poppy vibe to the band.

The group cut a five-song demo that was produced by Floyd Rose in Seattle, but Glass was not able to get signed to a label. However, one of the band's tracks, "Can't Be," was featured on a compilation, *KZOK: Best of the Northwest: 1983*. Glass fizzled after that, although the band never officially called it quits.

Around that time, Pilot was contacted by a hotshot guitarist, James Byrd, who wanted Pilot to sing on a demo recording in 1983. And this is when the story of Fifth Angel truly begins...

---

5. Ken Mary was doing session work as a drummer and finishing up high school at the time. A short while later, he was working with the band TKO and appears on the albums *In Your Face* (1984) and *Below the Belt* (1985).

Ed Sein, circa 1970. Photo courtesy of Ed Sein.

Ed Sein (left) with his first band in the backyard. Circa 1975.
Photo courtesy of Ed Sein.

A promotional photo of Ridge circa 1979-1980.
Photo courtesy of Ed Sein.

Ed Sein (left) and Ted Pilot (right) in 1977.
Photo courtesy of Ed Sein.

Ken Mary getting ready for Ridge band practice in 1977. Photo courtesy of Ed Sein.

Ed Sein upgrades his amplifier in 1977. Photo courtesy of Ed Sein.

Ted Pilot during Ridge band practice in 1977. Photo courtesy of Ed Sein.

Ed Sein performing at a Ridge show in 1978.
Photo courtesy of Ed Sein.

Ken Mary setting up his drums for a Ridge show in 1978.
Photo courtesy of Ed Sein.

Ridge before performing at an outdoor party in summer 1979. Photo courtesy of Ed Sein.

Ridge's rehearsal room in 1979. Photo courtesy of Ed Sein.

Ticket stubs from Ridge performances in 1979 and 1982.
Images courtesy of Ed Sein.

Ted Pilot singing live with Ridge, circa 1978-1980. Photo courtesy of Ted Pilot.

UNGAM P.O. BOX 33203   P.O. BOX 25008
SEATTLE, WA 98133   PORTLAND, OR 97225
(206) 776-3169   (503) 297-1581

THIS CONTRACT for the personal services of musicians on the engagement described below, made this __3rd__ __JULY__ 19 __79__, between the undersigned Purchaser of Music (herein called "Employer") and __FOUR__ musicians (including leader).

The musicians are engaged severally on the terms and conditions on the face hereof. The leader represents that the musicians already designated have agreed to be bound by said terms and conditions. Each musician yet to be chosen upon acceptance shall be bound by said terms and conditions. Each musician may enforce this agreement. The musicians severally agree to render services under the undersigned leader.

1. Name and Address of Place of Engagement __L.K. HILLS ROLLER RINK 16230 N.E 8th St__
   Print Name of Band or Group "__RIDGE__"
2. Interest, starting and finishing time of engagement __JULY 24, 1979   10:15 P.M. — 11:00 P.M__
3. Type of Engagement __BATTLE OF THE BANDS__
4. WAGE AGREED UPON: __$1.00 FOR EVERY COUPON RETURNED__

This wage includes expenses agreed to be reimbursed by the employer in accordance with the attached schedule, or a schedule to be furnished the Employer on or before the date of engagement.

5. Employer will make payments as follows: __IN FULL UPON CONCLUSION OF ENGAGEMENT__

6. The Employer shall at all times have complete supervision, direction, and control over the services of musicians on this engagement and expressly reserves the right to control the manner, means and details of the performance of services by the musicians including the leader as well as the ends to be accomplished. If any musicians have not been chosen upon the signing of this contract, the leader shall, as agent for the Employer and under his instructions, hire such persons and any replacements as are required.

The leader shall, as agent of the Employer, enforce disciplinary measures for just cause, and carry out instructions as to selections and manner of performance. The agreement of the musicians to perform is subject to proven detention by sickness, accidents, riots, strikes, epidemics, acts of God, or any other legitimate conditions beyond their control. On behalf of the Employer the leader will distribute the amount received from the Employer to the musicians, including himself as indicated on the opposite side of this contract, or in place thereof on separate memorandum supplied to the Employer at or before the commencement of the employment hereunder and take and turn over to the Employer receipts therefor from each musician, including himself. The amount paid to the leader includes cost of transportation, which will be reported by the leader to the Employer.

This contract cannot be cancelled except by mutual, written consent of both employer and leader.

All disputes are to be first negotiated through the agency, then, if not resolved, in a court of law.

The band shall be allowed two (2) fifteen-minute breaks for a three hour performance, three (3) fifteen-minute breaks for four hour performance, etc. Breaks shall not be within one-half hour of beginning or end of performance, except in case technical difficulties.

No performance on the engagement shall be recorded, reproduced or transmitted from the place of performance, in any form or by any means whatsoever, except by written agreement between employer and leader.

MUSICIANS

ED SEIN	
KEN MARY	
GREG KEENEY	
TED PILOT	

CRAIG COOKE   ED SEIN
Print Employer's Name   Print Leader's Name
X   X
P.O.   3
LYNNWOOD   98036   BELLEVUE   OR
City   Zip Code   City

The contract Ridge signed on July 3, 1979, to take part in the 1979 Battle of the Bands. (Some private information has been redacted.) Image courtesy of Ed Sein.

RIDGE

WILL ROCK THE
LAKE HILLS ARENA
THIS TUESDAY NIGHT
FOR THE CHAMPIONSHIP OF THE
1979 BATTLE OF THE BANDS!

IT'S A HIGH ENERGY
ROCK & ROLL CONCERT
YOU WON'T WANT TO MISS!*!

- ☐ AUGUST 28th (Tuesday)
- ☐ 9:30 p.m. – 1:30 a.m.
- ☐ LAKE HILLS 16232 N.E. 8th St. (Bellevue)
- ☐ $3.00 admission

FOR MORE INFO or $1.00 OFF TICKETS...
CALL 746-4625 or 453-9171

SPONSORED BY KISW & BANDWAGON MUSIC

One of the flyers Ridge used to promote their appearance at the 1979 Battle of the Bands. Image courtesy of Ed Sein.

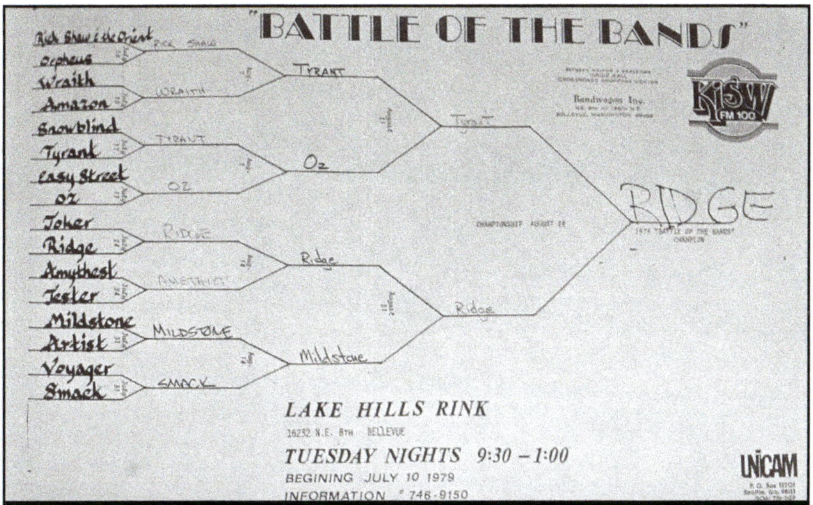

The bracket of bands that competed in the 1979 Battle of the Bands. Image courtesy of Brian L. Naron.

Some of the tickets used for the 1979 Battle of the Bands. Image courtesy of Ed Sein.

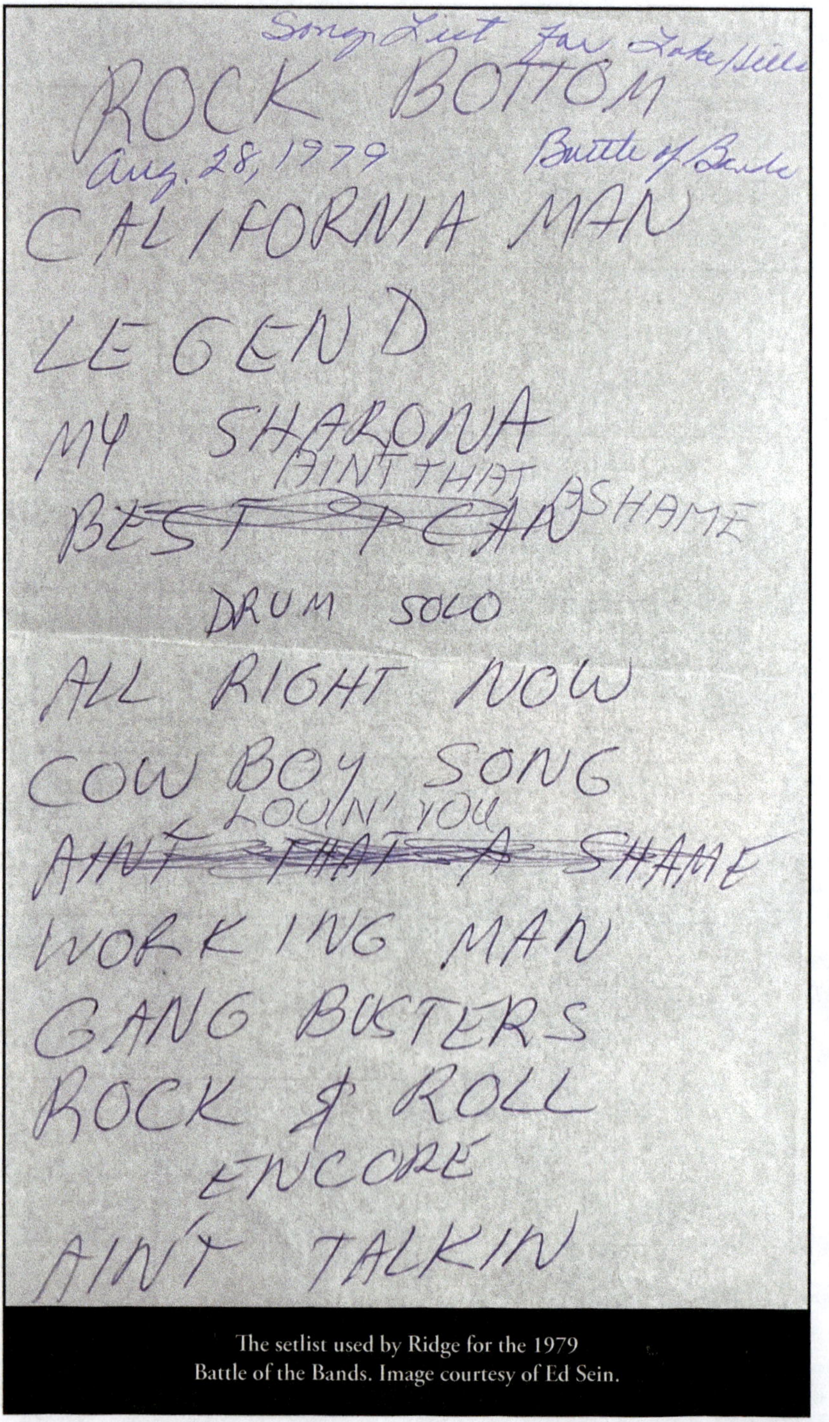

Song List for Lake/Hills

ROCK BOTTOM
Aug. 28, 1979 — Battle of Bands

CALIFORNIA MAN

LEGEND

MY SHARONA

BEST ~~I CAN~~ AIN'T THAT A SHAME

DRUM SOLO

ALL RIGHT NOW

COWBOY SONG

~~AIN'T THAT A SHAME~~ LOVIN' YOU

WORKING MAN

GANG BUSTERS

ROCK & ROLL

ENCORE

AIN'T TALKIN'

The setlist used by Ridge for the 1979 Battle of the Bands. Image courtesy of Ed Sein.

Crimson & Gray

Serving the Students of W. F. West High School Since 1913

Vol. LVII No. 9   W.F. West High School   Friday, January 25, 1980

Dance Tonight To Ridge After The Game

Darci Sabin Chosen 1980 DAR Good Citizen Award Receipent

By Mike Herren
News Editor

Twenty-one seniors were nominated for this year's Daughters of American Revolution Award. This award is given to a senior girl or boy who attends a public or private high school, and is a U.S. citizen.

Nominations for the award were based upon qualities of DEPENDABILITY - truthfulness, loyalty, punctuality, SERVICE - cooperation, courtesy, consideration of others, LEADERSHIP - personality, self-control, ability to assume control, and PATRIOTISM - unselfish interest in family, school, community, and nation.

The faculty nominated students who they felt held the qualities of a good citizen. This list was then distributed to the senior class who voted on the three candidates of their choice. The top three finalists were selected and then the faculty chose the 1980 DAR Good Citizen.

Seniors nominated for this year's contest were: Kenni Amrine, Tracey Anderson, Rocky Calkins, Pam Elder, Garth Johnson, Eunkyong Kim, Cara Knittle, Koni Kostick, Becky Locke, Ann Moody, Teri Mullins,

DARCI SABIN, 1980 DAR Good Citizen

Dave Nehring, Laura Prothero, Matt Roewe, Darci Sabin, Tracey Samson, Judy Stedham, Lori Ticknor, Tammy White, and Kim Wilson. Pam Elder, Darci Sabin and Kim Wilson were chosen by the senior class as the top three finalists. The faculty then chose Darci Sabin as the recipient of this year's DAR Good Citizen Award. Darci has taken an examination and completed a resume and application form.

Darci has been very active throughout her high school years. She is serving as secretary of her class, and holds membership in Honor Society, C Club, Pep Club and Pub Club. She is president of the Mixed Chorus, and is a member of Keysingers.

A tennis player, Darci is the only senior girl to participate in that sport for four years. She has earned two varsity letters. As a freshman, she received "The Most Improved Player Award". Her junior and senior years she was named "Team Inspiration".

After graduation from W.F. West, Darci plans to attend Centralia College, and then Western Washington University where she plans to major in Special Education.

Stephanie Connors, counselor who helped Darci with her state application, is very optimistic about Darci's chances to receive additional recognition. Mrs. Connors said, "Darci really exemplifies all the qualities that make a good citizen. In everything she does, she sets a fine example. She is concerned about others, and is eager to become involved in the affairs of the community. We are proud to have her represent our school."

Congratulations and good luck Darci.

Crimson and Gray Tour Publishing Company

Joan Ramsey
Staff Writer

Much more goes into publishing a newspaper than just writing stories, taking pictures, and setting up copy, as several Journalism students from W.F. West High School recently discovered.

On Tuesday, December 11, 1979, several members of the writing staff of the Crimson and Gray were given a tour through the Oregonian Publishing Company in Portland, Oregon.

The tour started at The Oregonian and Oregon Journal Press Building, where we saw a short filmstrip giving an overview of the things in store for us. The Press Building is where the actual printing of the newspaper takes place. The building occupies an entire city block and contains one of the largest printing presses on the West Coast.

Before the newspaper is printed, many things have to happen, one of which is the writing of stories. To learn about this we were taken to the Oregonian and Journal Building. It is not as big as the Press Building, but there is just as much activity going on under its roof.

Though most of the writers were busy preparing stories for the next issue of The Oregonian, we were able to talk to a few people of various departments. First, we talked with the Theatre Arts Critic, who writes a column giving her opinion of many of the plays, concerts, and films playing in the area.

Next, we spoke to the man in charge of selecting, and sometimes drawing, the political cartoons and the syndicated cartoons for the comic pages.

The Oregonian Editorial Department employs two writers, one of which writes primarily about tax information and government spending. The lady we visited with gives her opinions on humanitarian ideas and situations in the political area.

We also talked with one of the men in charge of Art Layout and Design. He is responsible for selecting and drawing the artwork used in the day edition of The Oregonian. He also helps select the artwork for the special section of The Oregonian, similar to the "Weekender" in the Daily Chronicle.

County Builds New Juvenile Facilities

The building being constructed near Green Hill School is the new Juvenile Detention Center for Lewis County. The facility should be ready for use in August, 1980. The juvenile center is for holding persons under 18 that are in trouble with the law until their parents can be notified or until they have a court appearance. The detention center is not part of Green Hill or the state, it is run by Lewis County.

There are several reasons for a new detention center, as the present building is on a 6½ year lease from the state which expires in June 1980. The state wants the building back because of limited space at Green Hill. The original building also has very limited office space and no recreation area for the kids.

The new building has an area of 13,020 square feet that will house a probation department, court room, office, 20 beds, a kitchen, a recreation area - that includes a basketball court, a classroom and a laundry room.

Ridge appearing on the front page of W.F. West High School's newspaper on Friday, January 25, 1980. Image courtesy of Ed Sein.

A flyer promoting Ridge's gig on May 2, 1980. Image courtesy of Ed Sein.

PM PRODUCTIONS PRESENTS

IN CONCERT

AT THE

SEATTLE CONCERT THEATRE

CORNER OF FAIRVIEW NORTH AND JOHN ST., 1 BLOCK OFF THE DENNY WAY EXIT

SAT. AUG. 21 - 8:30 pm

WITH SPECIAL GUEST

DON'T MISS THIS KICK ASS EVENT!

ADMISSION $3.25

3.75 AT THE DOOR

TICKETS AT ALL BASS OUTLETS

A flyer Ridge used to promote one of its summer shows. Image courtesy of Ed Sein.

At the Precipice

Ridge Triumphs at the 1979 Battle of the Bands

By Brett Miller[6]

In the mid-1970s, the rock scene in Bellevue, Washington, quietly welcomed a group of young musicians who would later take home one of the most talked-about victories in local music history. That band was Ridge, and their ambitious song repertoire struck a balance between heavy metal covers of acts such as Rush and Judas Priest, and the power pop of The Knack and Cheap Trick.

Ridge's origin was covered in more detail earlier in this book. But the band's deft understanding of the importance of accessibility proved crucial during the defining moment of their career: the 1979 Lake Hills Battle of the Bands.

Sponsored by UniCam, KISW, and Bandwagon, Inc., the Lake Hills Battle of the Bands was one of the most high-profile music competitions in the Pacific Northwest. Held at the Crossroads Lake Hills Roller

---

6. Brett Miller was a mainstay in the late-1970s and 1980s rock scene in the Pacific Northwest. He worked as a stage lighting manager and concert promoter, and eventually formed his own glam rock band, Lipstick, with the late Paul Passarelli.

Rink, in Bellevue, the event spanned six weeks, from July 10 to August 28, and featured 16 bands, many of which would go on to shape the region's rock and metal identity.

Ridge entered the fray on July 24, 1979, sharing the night's stage with Amethyst, Jester, and Joker. The latter group helped launch the careers of future Queensrÿche guitarists Chris DeGarmo and Michael Wilton. Ridge's performance included covers from local favorites Rail, UFO's "Rock Bottom," Cheap Trick's "My Sharona," and Ridge's own original track, "Screaming with Delight"—a Judas Priest-inspired rocker. Their blend of polish, power, and stage presence earned them a spot in the semifinals.

Two weeks later, Ridge advanced again—this time defeating a competitive lineup that included Amethyst, Smack, and Mildstone. That victory secured their place in the finals alongside their fiercest rival: Tyrant. Tyrant was no ordinary band. Their lineup featured Adam "Bomb" Brenner, a prodigious guitarist known for his mastering of the Edward Van Halen style of lead guitar, and a young singer named Jeff Tate, who would soon front Queensrÿche (and change his name to "Geoff"). Tyrant's music was heavier, louder, and less radio-friendly—but undeniably powerful.

The final showdown took place on August 28, 1979, and the show became the stuff of local legend. Ridge, tight and melodic, delivered a well-balanced set with clean sound engineering and strong audience rapport. Tyrant, on the other hand, suffered from volume issues—with Brenner reportedly cranking his Marshall amplifier too high, disrupting the overall mix. According to people at the shows, the Tyrant soundman was deaf in one ear, a detail that likely influenced the outcome. Ridge, however, spent some money to hire a qualified sound man who understood how to mix the sound for that venue.

The panel of judges—composed of music writers, school talent bookers, radio personalities, and industry insiders—ultimately named Ridge the winner of the 1979 Battle of the Bands. Not everyone accepted the result graciously. In interviews years later, Adam Bomb expressed frustration, alleging favoritism and claiming that Ridge had been set up to win. Tyrant disbanded the next day, its members citing internal disagreements and disappointment over the loss.

Ridge's drummer, Ken Mary, pushed back against the accusations, emphasizing that the band's professionalism and sound quality led to the win. Ridge had been together for several years, having played over a hundred shows by August 1979.

While the controversy still lingers in the memories of those who were there, the significance of that summer remains undeniable. The 1979 Battle of the Bands launched the careers of musicians who would shape rock and metal history—from Queensrÿche to Fifth Angel. For Ridge, the win symbolized not just victory, but validation.

Ridge started as kids jamming in a Bellevue garage and grew into a band that could command stages, captivate crowds, and win respect—if not always unanimous praise—from their peers. The group played all over the Pacific Northwest. Ridge's journey from junior high jam sessions to a legendary local title is a classic tale of talent, hustle, and heart.

Ridge performing at the 1979 Battle of the Bands.
Photos courtesy of Ed Sein.

"Safe in power they sit and wait. They can't understand their impending fate."

— Fifth Angel, "Call Out the Warning"

Chapter 2
Call Out the Warning

When James Byrd returned to Seattle from Los Angeles in the early 1980s, he had a clear vision of what he wanted to do—form a powerhouse group and get a major record deal. Byrd was committed to following the same strategy Queensrÿche used to capture the attention of EMI Records.

"[R]ather than expending energy playing gigs and trying to get record executives out to see the band, we'd hole up and self-finance a fully produced album and shop it," Byrd said.

"If you try to put together a band and play locally and make it that way around here, it's so destructive to your morale that eventually the band breaks up before it gets anywhere," Byrd added. "But when everybody in the band works as one cohesive unit with a mind toward, 'Let's make a great record; let's work in the basement until it's perfect; we're not doing anything until we've got a great product on tape,' then nobody's depressed about playing for 40 people in some rented roller rink somewhere."

Byrd's timing was perfect. By 1984, Pilot and Sein had a backlog of aggressive song ideas they couldn't use in Glass, and the duo wanted to get back to their hard rock and metal roots. Once Byrd contacted Pilot, things started to take shape.

Byrd initially got together with Pilot at a rehearsal space that that the guitarist had rented in the Green Lake neighborhood of Seattle. At the time, Byrd was enamored with Deep Purple, and was looking for a keyboardist for the band, particularly one with a Hammond B-3. That didn't pan out. It was around the third or fourth time Pilot and Byrd jammed when the latter remembers the singer asking him if Sein could join the fray. Byrd agreed, and in some ways, the union was kismet.

"I not only knew they had worked together, [but] I had actually once auditioned for the band they played in called Ridge, around 1981, if memory serves me about the date," Byrd said. "They ended up deciding they didn't want a second guitarist, and we went our separate ways."

Byrd added that he remembered Pilot being a student and Sein working for a local cable company at the time of Fifth Angel's inception.

"After listening to James play, I thought there was some definite potential there for a good songwriter and a great lead guitarist," Pilot said. "I called up Ken [Mary] and Ed Archer, who I, again, played with [in Ridge], and we got together. … Ever since that point, it really seemed to click. There was something there from the first day we all played together."

"Ted got together with James and came back and shared the material with me," Sein added. "It seemed compatible with our ideas, so we decided we should merge forces. Ted and I took some of James' ideas and made them better with ours."

Sein also transitioned to his stage name of Ed Archer during the early years of Fifth Angel. While most stage names are made up, "Archer" is the guitarist's actual true family name. His dad, Vic, changed his last name from "Archer" to "Sein," while he was living in Burma (now Myanmar), and kept it when he got married and immigrated to the United States. But Ed adopted "Archer" in Fifth Angel because, in addition to liking the European name better, he thought it had more meaning behind it, since it is his family's actual surname.

With Archer, Byrd, Mary, and Pilot firmly in place, Fifth Angel's earliest influences quickly surfaced. The group bonded over music from bands such as Iron Maiden, Judas Priest, Accept, Dio, and the Scorpions. In a nutshell, Fifth Angel focused on writing songs that concentrated on the melodic side of heavy metal.

"It's a blend of power and musicianship," Mary added, referring to Fifth Angel's first songs. "Each musician is great unto themselves, so there's no weak link."

The group rehearsed at the homes of both Byrd and Pilot during this time and started bantering around band names. After a bunch of non-starters, the guys were led to the Bible, specifically the Book of Revelation, by Ted's brother, Matt, who was taking a theology class at Pacific Lutheran University at the time.[7]

After initially scoffing at using the Bible to find a band name, Ed relented and started flipping through it and stumbled upon the story of the Fifth Angel, who holds the key to the abyss. And if the pit to the abyss is unlocked, havoc will be unleashed on the world. The tale's dark imagery and foreboding messaging resonated with the band, and "Fifth Angel" was selected as the group's moniker.

The first four tracks written by Fifth Angel were "Fade

---

7. Dr. Matt Pilot earned a Bachelor of Science in Biology from Pacific Lutheran University. He then attended the University of Washington School of Dentistry, graduating in 1990.

to Flames," "Fifth Angel," "Wings of Destiny," and "Under Pressure." These songs were composed mostly with acoustic guitars, according to Archer. This was because the bulk of the writing was done in Pilot's dad's basement. By using acoustic guitars, the band could hear each other well and really refine their parts. Fifth Angel captured their initial song ideas on simple cassette recorders.

Eventually, an eight-track demo (of all four songs performed with electric guitars) was made at Randy Hemming's studio, mostly for the band members to have something on tape to listen to and work on. Randy, who was a friend of the band, had a TEAC 8-track, reel-to-reel tape machine and a TEAC mixing board and various outboard gear and processing equipment.

"We knew Randy with Ridge and Glass, and basically the payment to Randy was in beer, specifically Canadian beer," Archer said, laughing. "Back in those days, it wasn't so easy to get. We paid him in cases, and he did our recording."

After some time and further song refinement, Fifth Angel was ready to hit a professional studio and record its official demo tape. The foursome toured various studios in the Seattle area and decided to record their songs at Steve Lawson Productions in Seattle. It was a 24-track studio, and an up-and-coming engineer at the time, Terry Date, recorded the sessions.

Date, who was previously an assistant under Tom Hall at Triad Studios, went on to fame working with Pantera, Dream Theater, Soundgarden and others. But at the time, he, like Fifth Angel, was just starting out. Date had engineered and co-produced Metal Church's self-titled debut album in 1984, which was originally released on Ground Zero, an independent label. Elektra Records snapped Metal Church up after that and reissued the album in 1985.

"It was really just a happenstance kind of thing with Terry," Archer said. "He was the head engineer at Lawson's, and he had experience with recording. Terry had a really good sounding demo reel of bands he'd recorded and knew his way around the mixing console. He was well versed with microphone placement and all the technical wizardry that goes on with professional audio recording."

Fifth Angel's 1984 demo was recorded as a quartet, with guitarist Archer also handling bass duties.[8] Once the recording was complete, the musicians were ecstatic about what they had created. Mary said that from their earliest jams and recording sessions, the band knew they had something special and were confident they would score a record deal. They sent the tape to every label they could think of and initially heard nothing. Eventually, an independent label, Shrapnel Records came calling.

Founded in 1980 by Mike Varney, Shrapnel was one of the first record companies in the United States to dedicate itself to the genre of heavy metal. Varney narrowed the label's focus over the next several years, looking to showcase the neo-classical electric guitar and shred styles, which aligned with James Byrd's lead guitar playing.

Once Varney got hold of Fifth Angel's tape, he was blown away by what he heard.

---

8. Bassist Randy Nelson (Ridge, Glass) was not asked to be a part of Fifth Angel. Archer said that at the time, they didn't need a bass player while the group wrote and recorded a demo. It wasn't until after Fifth Angel's album was completed that the band turned its attention to finding a bassist. And by that point, a lot of time had elapsed, and Nelson had moved on. Ultimately, Nelson went on to play with Adam Bomb, Heir Apparent, and several other groups.

"After hearing their demo, I immediately knew their potential was great. It was one of the best tapes I'd received," Varney said. "Part of the reason was, they'd spent lots of money doing it, whereas most bands don't. It sounded almost like a finished product. I couldn't believe any of the other labels didn't sign the band before I did."

Fifth Angel wasn't satisfied with being on an independent label, but at the time, they were thankful for the opportunity.

"[Y]ou're obviously limited to what you can do, you don't have things like tour support and things that you need to establish yourselves in the market, so we want to do things well on an independent level so that we can move on to a major which is where our goals are," Mary said, adding that Fifth Angel wants "to become the biggest heavy metal band in the world."

Varney inked Fifth Angel to a record deal in the United States, and Roadrunner Records came on board to put out Fifth Angel's self-titled debut in Europe. But the band had to finish the recording. Fifth Angel went back to work in 1985, writing "In the Fallout," "Shout it Out," "Call Out the Warning," "Only the Strong Survive," "The Night," and "Cry Out the Fools."

"The Night" was originally titled "I Will Return," a fact Archer had forgotten about. He rediscovered the song title change when he pulled out the initial contract between Varney and Fifth Angel, which listed all nine tracks on the band's first album. All the songs were written by Archer, Byrd, and Pilot as a trio, except for "Only the Strong Survive." Mary wrote the chorus of that track, helping shape the lyrics and melody.

Archer explained that Pilot's abilities as a guitar player really helped Fifth Angel flesh out their first songs.

"Ted understood the guitarist side of things in tandem

with the vocal side, and vice-versa with James and myself," Archer said. "Ted would come up with guitar riffs sometimes, and I'd share vocal ideas. It worked out well. We all had a very good musical rapport with each other in the beginning. We didn't always agree, but we were open-minded and would listen to each other's musical perspectives. Then we'd jam the songs with Ken as well and we'd all make any tweaks at that point."

Ed Archer (left) and Terry Date (right) working (goofing?) around in the studio while recording Fifth Angel's self-titled debut. Circa 1986. Photo courtesy of Ed Archer.

Eventually, Fifth Angel reconnected with Terry Date at Steve Lawson Productions and recorded the balance of the tracks that would complete their first album. Fifth Angel's recording sessions were mostly held on weekends and weekday evenings during off-hours. At the time, the studio was booked for recording TV and radio commercials during the day.

"I remember us running out of studio time and money, so we made a deal to get more time by having Terry listed as one of the producers," Archer said. "Our debut album was actually self-produced alongside Terry. I think at that time some of our ideas of adding in samples and trying things like putting exciters on cymbals and stereo bus compression may have been new ideas to him."

Archer used a variety of equipment to record his rhythm guitar tracks on *Fifth Angel*. He had a Marshall JMP 2204 Master Model Mk2 Lead 50-Watt Guitar Amp Head from 1978, and a Marshall 4x12 cabinet with Celestion greenback speakers. Archer also used a variac set to 140 volts, which the guitarist said was used on about half the album. Archer also built his own pre-amp/signal-boost circuit, which was used (without the variac) for the second set of songs recorded at Steve Lawson Productions.

The dedication of each member of Fifth Angel to get their parts "perfect" is perhaps best exemplified in a story about James Byrd. According to Pilot, Fifth Angel ran out of money for the recording, and Byrd wasn't quite satisfied with his lead section in "Cry Out the Fools." So, Pilot said Byrd sold his Marshall amplifier to the studio in exchange for more recording time so he could nail the guitar solo.

"He went back to Steve Lawson's and spent hours on that lead," Pilot recalled. "I love that guitar lead. James was a very melodic guitar player and had a lot of passion."

"Wings of Destiny" was another track that really showcased Byrd's dedication to Fifth Angel's music. Known for his fleet fingers, Byrd laid back a bit on that song's guitar solo, looking to enhance the emotional delivery of Pilot.

"That track needed to have an intimate feel and focus the listener on the lyric, and the story being told, which I felt was very powerful," Byrd said. "I wanted the vocal to have the last word. It needed to be a plaintive, sorrowful, and thought-provoking piece of music, and a bunch of unnecessary fast notes just wouldn't have done the track justice."

Archer and Pilot worked closely on the latter's vocal takes. The duo developed a meticulous and methodical system of recording songs line by line, and at times, word by word, punching in and out to make sure they got the best performances.

Some evenings, they would get through an entire song, and on other days, only the verses would be completed, and they would return the next night to do the choruses. It was frustrating for Pilot at times, but at the end of the day, they agreed that the results of their work made for a better album.

"Ted's vocals were produced by me, which sounds kind of pompous, but it's the truth," Archer said. "I started doing that when we were recording the demos at Randy Hemming's. And that continued at Steve Lawson's. At this point in time, Ted had been studying under Maestro David Kyle for a while, and his singing ability was getting better and more developed. But at times, there could be some pitchiness with certain phrases. I would be the ears for Ted, and he trusted me to do that."

But the sessions weren't always so serious. Some fun was had, particularly in the tape and duplication room at the studio.

"Ed and I spent some time back there recording words and playing them backwards," Mary recalled. "Then we would try to learn them, say them backwards and record them with the machine moving forwards. Then we'd flip the tape and play it backwards again to see if we could make it sound like you had said the word correctly. I know it sounds complicated, but basically, we were trying to say words reversed and then reverse them again to play normally. We had some pretty good laughs. A couple times we probably cried we were laughing so hard."

FIFTH ANGEL

The first promotional photo of Fifth Angel. From left to right: Kenny Kay, Ed Archer, Ted Pilot, James Byrd, and Ken Mary.

The promotional photo of Fifth Angel after the band signed with Shrapnel Records. From left to right: Ed Archer, Ken Mary, Ted Pilot, Kenny Kay, and James Byrd.

Kenny Kay, who was listed as the bass player on *Fifth Angel*, and appeared in promotional photos, was never a member of the band. Kay was just a stand-in to make it look like Fifth Angel was a complete group. Kay did not lay down the bass tracks on *Fifth Angel*. Ed Archer played the bass on the initial set of songs and Randy Hansen, known for his tribute band honoring Jimi Hendrix, recorded bass on the remaining tunes.[9]

The connection with Kay stemmed from his involvement with Ken Mary. The drummer played for Randy Hansen, and then later TKO. Kay was originally Ken Mary's drum technician with Hansen and was the band's front of house sound engineer. When Mary transitioned to TKO, Kay joined him, performing the same roles. Kay was asked by one of the guys in Fifth Angel to pose for the band photo as their bassist, and Kay was happy to do it.

Kay signed a release form for his photo for just $1, and that was the extent of his involvement with the band. A year or two down the road, when Fifth Angel was asked in an interview about what happened to Kay, the band stated that Kay simply lost interest in playing music. Kay was adamant that was not true. Kay has been a multi-instrumentalist (guitar, bass, keyboards) since he was 14 years old, and to this day, still writes and plays his own music.

"I was like, 'What the fuck are they talking about,'" Kay

---

9. When Fifth Angel was looking for a bass player to record the remaining tracks on their record, Tim Branom submitted a tape for the band to consider. While Branom was a friend and becoming quite a talented singer and musician in his own right, Fifth Angel ultimately decided to go with the more experienced Randy Hansen for the recording.

said. "It was disheartening, but I knew they were trying to sidestep the fact they didn't have a bass player. Back then, your image was everything and your first presentation and all that shit was so important."

The track "Under Pressure," which was one of the first songs written by Fifth Angel, did not end up on the album. The demo of "Under Pressure" eventually surfaced online, however, and readers interested in hearing it can likely find it on YouTube.

Archer and Byrd traded off guitar solos on "Under Pressure," making the tune an interesting listen. Byrd went back and relistened to the song in 2025, and felt it had a blues structure to it that didn't quite mesh with the band's vision for its music at the time.

"What sticks out to me the most is the lack of build and melody in the lead vocal during the choruses," Byrd said. "It could have been a much better track, but even if it was better, it still doesn't fit the approach of the rest of the album."

Fifth Angel were unified in their goal to make an album that had no filler tracks. Simply put, "Under Pressure" did not make the grade.

"Call Out the Warning," the third cut on *Fifth Angel*, is a prime example of a band firing on all creative cylinders, however. Byrd said that he brought in the music to the song's chorus, the chorus vocal melody, and the music in the song's bridge. Archer wrote the music of the verses, and Pilot took care of the lyrics and the rest of the vocal melodies.

"The band really has to be given a lot of credit because the album was pretty much produced by us," Mary confirmed. "We arranged all the songs, wrote all the music and, as a matter of fact, when the mixes didn't come out right, we actually took money out of our own pockets and went back and remixed it."

Initially, Varney wanted the album mixed by someone else. Fifth Angel relented, but when the initial mixes came back, the band wasn't satisfied, and Varney allowed Fifth Angel to do it themselves at Steve Lawson Productions. *Fifth Angel* was mastered by George Horn at Fantasy Studios, in Berkeley, California.[10]

Fifth Angel was incredibly proud of their first record, which was released on September 15, 1986. At the time, Mary called it one of the strongest albums to come out of Seattle aside from the albums issued by Queensrÿche and Metal Church.

"I think we wanted to establish a band identity and musically we were very pleased with the outcome, considering the budget and constraints of time," Mary said. "All the songs are great tracks—we put everything we had into them."

The front and back covers of *Fifth Angel*, autographed by Ken Mary, Ed Archer, James Byrd, and Ted Pilot, to the author.

10. Fantasy Studios permanently closed on September 15, 2018. Ironically, the date was the 32nd anniversary of the release of *Fifth Angel*.

Most of the heavy riffs and melodic arrangements on *Fifth Angel* are thanks to Byrd and Archer. Archer said for the most part, he played all rhythm guitar tracks on the album. But the guitar performances are heightened by the creativity, speed, and dexterity of James Byrd. Byrd's guitar solos on the nine songs are often compared to those written and played by legendary guitarist Yngwie Malmsteen. Malmsteen even shared some rare public praise for Byrd's playing, calling him "One of the best European sounding guitarists" he had heard, who "aims for each note and makes it count."

Ted Pilot's powerhouse delivery shines throughout the album, his voice reminiscent of a cross between Ronnie James Dio and Don Dokken, while Ken Mary's powerful groove, timing, and adaptability provide the foundation on which *Fifth Angel* was built. The group also played around with synthesizers to give the album a broader sound.

"We discovered sampled keyboards," Mary said. "They had a Kurzweil we ended up using for some background choir on 'Cry Out the Fools.' We couldn't believe how great the samples sounded. Back then, the technology was just beginning to emerge, and it was kind of like magic to us."

Archer said he remembered discovering the Kurzweil when he was killing time strolling through Steve Lawson Productions' keyboard room. He started playing around with certain sounds, and like Mary said, some of it found its way to "Cry Out the Fools" and various other tracks on the album.

One of those other tracks to feature a synthesizer was the band's namesake song, "Fifth Angel." The 10-second part appears from :23-:33 in the song and is performed by Ron Stokes, who used a Sequential Circuits Prophet-10 synthesizer.[11] According to band friend and fellow musician Tim Branom, at the time of the recording, Stokes' band, Uncle Sam, was also in the studio, and Fifth Angel asked Stokes to guest on the track.

Fifth Angel is not a traditional concept album where the lyrics form a story. But there is a unifying theme that explores the stark realities of faith, fate, and the threat of global annihilation through nuclear war. Pilot was careful not to make any religious statements (given the origin of the band's name) but consciously focused on writing about subjects in a different or unusual way, deliberately incorporating "mystical content" into the songs.

For example, one of Pilot's favorite tracks from the record is "Cry Out the Fools," which he said has all the emotion, melody, and intensity that help define a great song.

"I wrote about things that affect me emotionally, that's something special I try to put across in a song," Pilot said. "But I don't think any song should be too obvious. I like them to mean five or six different things to five or six different people."

"I love the song still, and this song's lyrics are perhaps more meaningful to me now than when we were young," Ken Mary added.

In recent years, most of the band members still feel like the songs and production on *Fifth Angel* have held up, and apart from the sound being overly compressed (a trait of

---

11. Sequential Circuits was an American synthesizer company founded by Dave Smith in 1974. The company released the first programmable polyphonic synthesizer in 1978 (the Prophet-5). The Prophet-10 (which was larger and featured two keybeds) was released a few years later.

the era) the record stands the test of time. Byrd was not quite as positive in his assessment of the record, although he admitted that was chiefly because of his perfectionist nature.

The guitarist said that time and budget restrictions resulted in him only having about 45 minutes per track to cut his guitar solos and other lead spots, which did not give him time to improvise and experiment with new ideas. In addition, Byrd was not impressed with the sound on the album.

Byrd explained that he did not use his usual set up for the recording that he had established for himself in 1981. The guitarist explained that his tone "lacked sparkle and mid-range focus," and he did not care for the chorus added to his guitar, even though it was his idea during mixdown of the record.

"I do think the album is really, really good, and I'm not unhappy with anything I played," Byrd said. "It's just that it can always be better."

Ken Mary perhaps sums up the band's thoughts on Fifth Angel's debut record best.

"For how young we were and the effort we put forth to try to create an amazing album, I'm very proud of what we accomplished," Mary said. "I think it sounds very professional for its era, because of the musicianship and the attention to detail in the songwriting, recording, and performances. The lessons of creating that album followed me through life, actually. Whatever you're going to do, do it with excellence."

The album cover of the Shrapnel Records version of *Fifth Angel* is just as striking as the music. A winged monster arises from the depths of a wasteland on post-apocalyptic Earth, as the fifth angel, holding a key, floats in shadow nearby. Ed Archer came up with the concept, which was brought to life by painter Guy Aitchison.[12]

Once Fifth Angel's self-titled debut was released, Pilot said there was some early negativity surrounding it. The singer recalled people in the southern United States mistakenly thinking Fifth Angel was a Satanic band and burning the record. But the album's reception quickly turned positive.

The late Malcolm Dome spotlighted Fifth Angel in *Kerrang!* And Dave Reynolds wrote up a piece on the group in *Metal Forces*. In addition, college radio stations in the United States were playing Fifth Angel's songs, which created a buzz in the heavy metal world. The hype was real.

"'Shout it Out' may be pounding and anthemic, but it somehow steers clear of Mötley Crüe's thud-rock banality and emerges as the kind of hymn to pillage and burn by; you can almost envision Viking hordes emerging from the mist," wrote KJ Doughton.

Adrianne Stone remarked that *Fifth Angel* "has all the melodic strength of Judas Priest and the power punch of Iron Maiden." Stone's sentiments were shared by many in the media. Dome said the record was filled with "ripping chords" and "anthemic pinnacles" throughout tracks such as "The Night," "Shout It Out," "In the Fallout," "Fade to Flames" and "Call Out the Warning."

"The point is that Fifth Angel could turn out to be

---

12. Aitchison and Fifth Angel connected through Shrapnel Records. The artist started his career illustrating album covers in 1985. Aitchison later became a tattoo artist and gave singer/songwriter/movie director Rob Zombie his first tattoo in 1989. Aitchison and his wife, artist Michele Wortman, are the owners of Hyperspace Studios in Marion, Ill.

something of a real gem, sparkling all the way along the road to an outpocket called greatness," Dome wrote in November 1986. "Their style draws heavily from both the rage and passion of Euro-Metal and also the more structured tonal attitudes of the Americans, with the razorpoint twin attack of guitarists Ed Archer and James Byrd (the latter a true find) lying fallow under the astonishingly vulturine vocals of Ted Pilot. Yeah, a special band are Fifth Angel."

The band was very aware of all the positive press their album was getting.

"We're getting a lot of fan mail from around the U.S. and overseas from people who've heard the record on the air," Byrd said at the time.

Fifth Angel was elated at the early success its record was having. But the band wanted more. Specifically, the group was hellbent on securing a major label recording contract. But before Fifth Angel could really reach the mountaintop and score a lucrative deal, they needed a permanent bass player.

Concept drawings for the cover art of *Fifth Angel*.
Images courtesy of Ed Archer.

Early sketches of the elements that would later appear on the cover of Fifth Angel's first album. Images courtesy of Ed Archer.

Early black and white concept art for *Fifth Angel*. Images courtesy of Ed Archer.

The original cassette version of *Fifth Angel* on Shrapnel Records.
Note the incorrect track sequence on the cover.

In His Words

James Byrd on His Endorsement Deal with Ibanez

Mike Varney asked me who I wanted an endorsement with, and he had offers from a bunch of guitar companies right after we signed with him. I was very much thinking as a businessman, in addition to being a musician, and although I thought that Ibanez was making the best quality instruments at the time, they actually didn't make a guitar I was interested in.

    Ibanez told him they would make whatever I wanted in their custom shop, and Mike advised me to go with Ibanez, because they were willing to put money into advertising, and I wanted to do everything I could to ensure the Fifth Angel album was going to be successful. Ibanez was terrific, and they made me some fantastic guitars, which I continued to use on many solo albums after *Fifth Angel* was released.

    When it was time to do the advertisements, they wanted me to appear in ads with an RG550, but I made them install three single-coil sized DiMarzio HS2 pickups in it, because I did not want to advertise something I did not play. They put my pickup configuration into every guitar they sent me, and I was quite upfront about it from the beginning. I think they probably sent me a dozen guitars between 1986 and 1993, and all but one were modified or completely custom, from their custom shop. The only one that wasn't, was a Lonestar electric nylon string they no longer made, but I had played one and liked it, and they actually went out and found a used one and bought it and sent it to me. That was some stellar treatment. They really believed in me.

Speaking of the ad, there was an incident on my trip to Ibanez. I was flown out to Pennsylvania for four days for that, and the plane I was on went into a very severe thunderstorm. During the descent to land, shit was flying everywhere, service carts, stewardesses, luggage, food, and then in the middle of that, it was struck by lightning. I thought a bomb had gone off. There was a blinding flash, and a deafening boom, and instantly, the lights went off, and the engines died. We plummeted in complete blackness for what seemed like forever, but if I had to estimate, it was probably only 30 seconds. But people were crying, praying quietly, some were screaming in terror, groaning in pain. When the lights came back on, there were flight attendants with bloodied faces, one lying face down in the aisle. People were carried off in stretchers before we were allowed to disembark.

I had gotten on that flight having not slept the night before, and I was absolutely shattered and exhausted when I was picked up at about 11 p.m. I went straight to makeup for two hours, and then to the ad photo shoot, which was in an alley in a very bad part of Philadelphia, which began at around 2 a.m. The thunderstorm was still raging. They had set up plastic and tarps between the rooftops, because the downpour was absolutely torrential, and more than once, the plastic got blown off, breached by the wind. The people living in the apartments on either side of the alley were not happy with the incredibly bright lights, and every time the even brighter flash bulbs went off with a shot, they would open their windows and swear at us.

That first night in Philadelphia was utterly surreal, and in the photo, I think I looked like someone who was in a state of shell shock, because I pretty much was. You can see the dark circles under my eyes in that photo. That photo session didn't end until it was starting to get light out. It was one of the most insane nights of my life. Anyway, the rest of my visit with Ibanez was fantastic, and Rich Lasner, the head of artist relations, was an absolute prince of a guy.

The Ibanez advertisement featuring James Byrd that appeared in *Guitar World*.

From the Congregation

How an Early Believer Discovered Fifth Angel

By Brian L. Naron[13]

One of my favorite record stores back in the 1980s was a place called Penny Lane Records. They had two locations: one in West Seattle, and another one in Lakewood, Washington. The Lakewood store was the one I frequented the most. The owner of both stores was Willie Mackay, the original manager of Metal Church. The store specialized in hard rock/heavy metal and rap, especially artists from the Northwest. They also hosted the first in-store autograph sessions with Queensrÿche and Culprit in 1983. It was at the Lakewood store where I first heard Fifth Angel.

Tony Sibonga had worked for the store for quite a while, and he loved all kinds of music. He made it his mandate to inform his customers about the music the store was selling. Once he knew what I liked he would hand me a couple of records and say, "Check these out at the listening station, you'll love 'em!" In September

---

13. Brian L. Naron is co-owner of Northwest Metalworx Music, an independent record label that specializes in unearthing lost Pacific Northwest hard rock and heavy metal bands.

1986, Tony handed me the store copy of Fifth Angel's self-titled debut album. I put that record on the turntable and listened to "In the Fallout" and was immediately struck by their power, Ted Pilot's voice and those big guitar sounds of James Byrd and Ed Archer. I was aware of Ken Mary's bombastic drums from the other Northwest bands he had been in. I put the stylus down on a couple more songs, but truth be told, I was sold on the band immediately. I bought my copy, and Tony also gave me the band's press kit and promo photo (which I still own).

I made a Xerox copy of the pink merchandise sheet from the first Fifth Angel album and mailed off my money order for a T-shirt and autographed photo. Several weeks later my money order was returned with a note stating that the merchandise was not yet ready and that a postcard would be sent out later with details. That postcard never arrived and so I wondered if Fifth Angel would ever play live or sell merch.

The front image of the first Fifth Angel T-shirt.

It took some time—almost 31 years—but finally, on April 22, 2017, I finally got to see Fifth Angel play a hometown show in Seattle (at El Corazón) and I was able to buy my T-shirt. Better late than never!

 **MERCHANDISE**

FIFTH ANGEL "ARMAGEDDON" ENLISTMENT
1 Year, $15.00 Membership Includes:

FREE FIFTH ANGEL TOUR 86-87 T-SHIRT

* Quarterly newsletter * Band Photo (Personally autographed by the ENTIRE group) * Discounts on FA merchandise * Tour information * Record information * Band Biography   COST: $15.00 EA

FOR EACH MEMBERSHIP PLEASE INCLUDE FOUR (4) SELF ADDRESSED STAMPED ENVELOPES

FIFTH ANGEL "RIDING ON THE WINGS" TOUR 86-87 FASHIONS

T-SHIRTS: Full color two sides, on black shirt. 50/50 blend, 1st quality, made in U.S.A. (Small, Medium, Large) COST: $10.95 EA

HOODED SWEATSHIRTS: Full color two sides, on black long sleeve hooded sweatshirt. 50/50 blend, 1st quality, made in U.S.A. (Small, Medium, Large) COST: $19.95 EA

BASEBALL JERSEYS: Full color two sides, white shirt with black sleeves. 50/50 blend, 1st quality, made in U.S.A. (Small, Medium, Large) COST: $13.95 EA

MUSCLE SHIRT: Full color one side, on black muscle shirt. 50/50 blend, 1st quality, made in U.S.A. (Small, Medium, Large) COST: $9.95 EA

HALF SHIRTS: Full color both sides on gray half shirt, no sleeves. 50/50 blend, 1st quality, made in U.S.A. (Small, Medium, Large) COST: $8.95 EA

LADIES BLACK LACE PANTIES: Full color one side on ladies black lace panty. One size, made in U.S.A. COST: $4.95 EA

FIFTH ANGEL PERSONALLY AUTOGRAPHED PHOTOS

Black and white band photo, personally autographed by each band member. COST: $6.00 EA

Black and white band photo autographed by the member of your choice. COST: $3.00 EA

--- (cut here) ---

QUANTITY	CHECK ITEM	PRICE
	[ ] FIFTH ANGEL "ARMAGEDDON" ENLISTMENT (Check shirt size) S[ ] M[ ] L[ ]	
	[ ] T-SHIRT S[ ] M[ ] L[ ]	
	[ ] HOODED SWEATSHIRT S[ ] M[ ] L[ ]	
	[ ] BASEBALL JERSEY S[ ] M[ ] L[ ]	
	[ ] MUSCLE SHIRT S[ ] M[ ] L[ ]	
	[ ] HALF SHIRTS S[ ] M[ ] L[ ]	
	[ ] LADIES PANTIES	
	[ ] BAND PICTURE FULLY AUTOGRAPHED	
	[ ] BAND PICTURE AUTOGRAPHED BY (MARK CHOICE): Ted Pilot [ ] James Byrd [ ] Ed Archer [ ] Kenny Mary [ ] Kenny Kay [ ]	
	Inside North America add $1.50 shipping	
	Outside North America add $3.50 importing	
	(Please print clearly)	TOTAL

SEND CHECK OR MONEY ORDER (U.S. CURRENCY ONLY) TO:

PM PRODUCTIONS
P.O. BOX 40298
BELLEVUE, WA. 98004
U.S.A.

Please allow six (6) weeks for delivery. If order is accompanied by check, please allow additional two (2) weeks for check to clear. Outside North America allow additional one (1) week for shipping. MONEY ORDERS ARE PROCESSED IMMEDIATELY!

VOID WHERE PROHIBITED. Other Fifth Angel merchandise availible soon. Send self addressed, stamped envelope for advance availibility information.

 NAME
ADDRESS
CITY   STATE   ZIP
COUNTRY   PHONE # (optional)

Fifth Angel's first merchandise sheet.
Image courtesy of Brian L. Naron.

> "They stand hand in hand.
> At the dawn of Fifth Angel."
>
> - Fifth Angel, "Fifth Angel"

Chapter 3
Making the Climb

John Macko was born in December 1958, in Los Angeles. He grew up on a cul-de-sac in Thousand Oaks, a city in Ventura County, California. John was interested in music early in his life and remembers his mother buying him a 45 RPM record of "Yesterday" by the Beatles.

John's parents divorced when he was a teenager, and he lived with his father, who was a firefighter. Due to the 24-hour shifts worked by firefighters, John and his brother were left by themselves for long stretches of time and listened to numerous records. Eventually, neighborhood friends came over and music turned into a passion, and eventually, a desire to be in a band.

"My buddy Tom was already playing guitar, and then another friend, Chuck, had an interest in playing drums," Macko said. "They're like, 'Okay, John, well, you've got to go play bass.' I didn't care, and that's how I started playing bass. But I was also playing guitar because my dad had an acoustic guitar I would fiddle around on."

Macko's first bass was nothing special. His father used to attend Sunday swap meets in Southern California. One day he brought home a cheap bass guitar and small amplifier for John. But the budding musician didn't have to wait long for an upgrade. Eventually, Macko was able to convince his dad to buy him a short-scale Fender Mustang Bass, and a small combo amplifier.

By the time Macko was in high school, he was playing in several amateur groups. When he was a senior, John picked up a Fender Jazz Bass, and he started to get plenty of opportunities to play around town.

"There were a lot of musicians and then everybody would float around and play in these garage bands," Macko said. "I did that for a number of years."

After high school, John stopped playing music regularly. He was working full-time in the construction field, doing framing and carpentry. After a few years of grinding out the stereotypical nine-to-five lifestyle, John reconnected with his buddy Tom, and they started playing in a lounge band. Now age 21, Macko realized he could make good money playing music and tried his hand as a professional musician.

Macko mostly played pop music with Tom for about six months. Then another friend, Frank, who was a keyboard player in a traveling cover band called Wheels, wanted to add a guitar player and a bass player. John and Tom jumped at the chance to join.

"That was the catalyst that really pushed me from a garage band level into more of what I would consider a professional level," Macko said. "Playing with higher standard musicians who were older, more experienced, and really good. They taught me how to play, and how to play tight, and how to dress, how to stand, how to grow my hair, everything. Even the clothes I wore on stage."

Wheels toured extensively in the Pacific Northwest, playing pop standards and radio hits. The band would gig throughout Washington, Idaho, Oregon, Wyoming, and even make the trek up to Alaska. Wheels would go up to Alaksa for four-month stays. The group would also play Honolulu, Hawaii, for extensive periods of time.

John honed his skills as a bass player as a member of Wheels, as he was on stage for multiple sets, playing six nights per week. During that time, Macko got to know members of the Carmel Watters Band. The group was from Seattle, and they needed a bass player. John accepted their offer and relocated from California to Seattle in 1985. The Carmel Watters Band performed some original songs, along with cover tunes. Macko played with them for quite some time, eventually moving on to join another group from Seattle, The Machine. That band gave John an opportunity to record music in the studio, which would come in handy shortly.

Like most working musicians, John frequented local music stores. One of the sales guys in the bass department of American Music in the Ballard neighborhood of Seattle was Richard Gibson of Myth. At some point in 1987, John said Richard tipped him off that Fifth Angel was looking for a bass player, and that the band was on the verge of signing a record contract with a major label. Gibson connected Macko with Ed Archer, and the two agreed to meet.

Macko had not heard of Fifth Angel before, but with the prospect of the band getting a major label record deal, he jumped at the chance to audition. Archer stopped by Macko's apartment in Ballard to pick up John's demo tape, photos and other materials. Archer also dropped off a copy of Fifth Angel's debut album on Shrapnel Records. Once Archer left, John dropped the needle on the record and was intimidated by what he heard coming from the speakers.

"I didn't think I could play it, I had never played that kind of heavy music before," Macko recalled. "The fact that they actually wanted me to come in and audition—I was pretty shocked, because I just figured they'd listen to this pop bull crap I was doing and go, 'Next.' I know I would have."

Archer called Macko and said regardless of the bassist's lack of experience playing heavy metal, the guys in Fifth Angel could tell John was skilled and wanted him to learn four or five of the band's songs. Macko auditioned in the basement of guitarist James Byrd's house, where Fifth Angel rehearsed. According to Macko, the audition didn't go well.

"I came in and Ed had to show me a lot of the parts because I didn't have the parts right," Macko admitted. "I remember just being really nervous, and in all honesty, I was out of my league. I was not good enough to be in that band."

Archer remembers it differently, however, saying that he was impressed with Macko's ability from the get-go. He explained that he felt John's sense of timing locked-in well with Ken Mary, and Macko's new passion and enthusiasm for heavier music was appealing. Pilot recalled that Fifth Angel stopped auditions after Macko, because they knew they had their guy.

John was shocked when he got the call from Ed a week or so later, offering him the job. Macko believes he got the job with Fifth Angel initially because of his good looks, as opposed to his skill as a bass player. Archer didn't deny that Macko's image played a role in the decision, explaining that in the 1980s, image was always a consideration for a group looking to expand its fanbase.

Macko said that Ted, Ed, and Ken all agreed on selecting him as the bass player, but James Byrd wasn't happy with the decision.

"I know James' take on me was like, 'This guy fucking can't play' and I'm okay with that," Macko said. "I think it's funny because to be honest, I probably would have sided with

James. I knew I wasn't good enough. I saw it as an opportunity to raise the bar on my playing."

Eventually, however, Macko's skill level rose to a point where he felt confident that his abilities matched those of the other players in Fifth Angel. It took about two years of practicing and working on technique before he was comfortable playing metal at the level of his bandmates. But in the interim, Fifth Angel had found its bass player, and signing with a major label seemed imminent for the band.

Fifth Angel rehearsed regularly throughout 1986 and into 1987. Most of the members were either working, going to school, or pursuing other musical interests (or a combination of all three). Archer and Pilot even formed their own production company, Nightsong Productions, to help other young bands develop their sound and navigate the local music scene.[14]

Fifth Angel's debut album eventually caught the ear of Derek Simon with Concrete Management, Inc., in New York. Founded by Bob Chiappardi and Walter O'Brien in 1984, the company's first client was the band Grim Reaper, and they later worked with Chrysalis Records on Armored Saint's full-length debut, *March of the Saint*.

According to Pilot, Simon's industry connections were a huge factor in Fifth Angel deciding to work with him. Archer noted that Simon and the band had a "handshake agreement" that Concrete would represent Fifth Angel if they were able

---

14. For example, Archer and Pilot helped mix the 1989 demos of a local band called Gypsy Rose, which featured singer/guitarist Tim Branom.

to score the band a record deal with one of the major labels. The guitarist added that there was a kinship between Simon and Fifth Angel, as they were all young and looking to make a name for themselves in the music business.

"He was an up-and-coming manager and we, as musicians had this dream of being successful in the music industry and making a living at it," Archer said. "Derek, in a parallel path, wanted to be successful in the music industry in a different capacity. It just worked."

Simon quickly went to work on Fifth Angel's behalf. He contacted numerous labels, and eventually hit paydirt with Epic Records, a subsidiary of the Columbia Records unit of CBS. At the time, Epic was soaring as a company, having released *Thriller* (1982) and *Bad* (1987) by Michael Jackson. Both albums were eventually certified Diamond by the Recording Industry Association of America (RIAA) in several countries for sales above 10 million.[15]

Bob Feineigle[16] from Epic Records flew to Seattle and watched Fifth Angel rehearse in Byrd's basement. As Archer explained, the band's practice space there was spacious, comfortable, and most importantly, it sounded good. They had floor wedges, sidefills, carpeted floors, and soundproofing. It was an ideal location for a showcase gig.

---

15. Michael Jackson's *Thriller* has sold more than 70 million copies worldwide since its debut.

16. Bob Feineigle was a director of A&R (artists and repertoire) for Epic Records in the 1980s. He primarily supervised A&R activities of East Coast-based artists (Fifth Angel notwithstanding). He was also a liaison with CBS Records International's U.K. company in coordinating activities such as new artist signings and product releases.

"Bob was hanging out, listening to what we're playing live, rocking out, and it was pretty cool," Archer said. "That's the showcase where we actually played live for someone other than ourselves, family or close friends."

Satisfied that Fifth Angel could truly play their material, negotiations with the label began. The process took a long time, with Archer explaining that their attorney, Barry Slotnick, went back and forth repeatedly with Epic, trying to secure the best deal for Fifth Angel. It took quite a bit of time to hammer out the deal, which ended up as a seven-album contract, with escalating recording budgets for each successive record.

Once Fifth Angel signed with Epic, they also signed an official management contract with Concrete in March 1988, retroactive to July 1987. The ball was finally in motion and things were proceeding at full speed for the band. The group was excited about their future, hoping to conquer the rock scene with the promotional and financial muscle of a major label behind them.

"The reason I think we got signed is because of the strength of our songs," Pilot said. "We have a good melodic content to our material, and I think that's important. We tried to keep a good diversity in the songs that went on the album."

"We worked really hard at making the record as good as it could be," Mary added. "And it paid off."

Yet, while Fifth Angel was on the cusp of achieving one of their career goals, personality conflicts between some of the band members threatened to destroy all that they had worked for.

The chemistry between the band and James Byrd was breaking down. According to Archer, once Fifth Angel started getting praise and good press, Byrd became frustrated at the band's decision-making process, particularly when issues weren't decided in the way he thought they should be. Subsequently, Byrd allegedly started threatening, on more than one occasion, to leave the band, which frustrated the other members of Fifth Angel.

"I really didn't have a relationship with him," Macko said of Byrd. "He ignored me, from what I remember. I had a lot of respect for him because I thought he was an amazing player. As a person, what struck me about him—and I didn't know him like the other guys did—was he was very opinionated. He was very critical and not open-minded."

At some point, Pilot recalled manager Derek Simon suggesting to the band that if they were concerned about Byrd and wanted someone new, that they should do it before Fifth Angel started traveling extensively. Discussing the issue in early 2025, Simon said he is sure he and Ted had that conversation, but the manager was adamant that he would not have initiated a move to get rid of Byrd.

"I think that there was some consensus within the band that it was time to move on from him," Simon said, regarding Byrd. "It was about him driving most of us crazy. I remember just these long painstaking conversations with James at least a couple of nights a week. He wasn't someone that the band wanted to be around. He was just really difficult. Maybe if we had all been on the road together, everything would have sort of settled down; the work and building the base would have become the focus. But when it was a lot of everyone sitting at home doing their thing and waiting for things to happen, James wasn't a great person to be around at that stage."

Moving on from Byrd was a difficult issue for everyone.

As a result, it took a bit of time before the matter was resolved. Pilot added that at some point, the band decided to call Byrd's bluff on leaving, and the singer was the one who told Byrd that he was out of the Fifth Angel.

"It's not like James did anything horrible, or anything like that," Pilot said. "It's like a relationship—you either grow together or you grow apart. It was as simple as that. Over time, as people started to mature a little bit more and our personalities diverged, he just didn't quite mesh with everybody."

Archer said it was also partly about reliability, recalling discussions with Pilot and Simon that if Byrd kept threatening to quit Fifth Angel, it may disrupt a recording schedule, or perhaps touring. In their view, a less volatile personality would benefit the band in the long term.

Byrd, however, saw things quite differently. He has said on numerous occasions that he was outright fired from the band. In addition, Byrd said that Archer and Pilot reneged on an original agreement between the three of them to split the songwriting publishing royalties equally at 33.33 percent per song, regardless of who wrote what.

"It was actually very generous from my end because I wrote the majority of the music on *Fifth Angel*," Byrd said.

Pilot and Archer disagree completely with Byrd's statement, saying that it was the two of them that wrote the lion's share of the record's songs, not Byrd, despite what the credits in the album liner notes may indicate.

In any event, Byrd claims once Concrete started managing the band, and a major label deal with Epic was in place, Archer and Pilot gave Byrd an ultimatum. He could either sign a new agreement that gave Archer and Pilot the majority of the band's publishing, or the duo would walk away from the record deal. Byrd described it as "financial blackmail."

"I signed the new agreement under their threat to destroy the deal with management and CBS," Byrd said. "After signing it, it was the last communication I ever had with either of them. Two weeks after I signed it, I received a notice from Concrete management that I was fired."

Ken Mary was busy touring with other bands at the time and wasn't directly involved in the situation. But he recalled there being a tremendous amount of friction between Archer, Byrd, and Pilot. So, he wasn't surprised when Byrd was gone.

"Could they have handled it better? Probably," Ken said. "There's always deals that can be made. But it did seem to me that they just couldn't get along."

Despite the serious nature of the discussions regarding Byrd, there was a moment of levity, at least amongst Simon, Pilot, Archer, and Macko. Simon remembers taking Fifth Angel to dinner in early 1988 at Genghis Cohen, a New York City-style Chinese restaurant in Los Angeles. The matter of Byrd's status in Fifth Angel had been discussed in private already, and they had decided to move on from Byrd once promotion of the first album was finished. But he was still in the band at this point.

"As we're getting the check, they bring these fortune cookies to the table," Simon said. "We're going around the table and reading our fortunes to everybody else. We get to James, and his fortune is 'Hope for the best, but expect the worst.' Obviously, it is generic Chinese fortune cookie fodder. But when you're sitting with a band, and you're going to ask somebody to leave, and that person reads that as their fortune, I think all of us tried to be still, but I remember moving my eyes to some of the other guys, just like, 'What the fuck?!' It was one of those moments."

Ultimately, when Pilot told Byrd he was out of Fifth Angel, the guitarist did not take the news well. Simon remembers Byrd being incredulous, wondering how he could be kicked out of a group that he worked to build up.

"I recall there being shock and then anger from James," Simon said. "He was with a band on a major label, and then all of a sudden, he wasn't. He didn't go quietly. He didn't get into lawsuits or threats, but he definitely tried to stake his claim."

With respect to all parties involved, whichever point of view is ultimately correct, the fact of the matter was, Byrd was out of Fifth Angel, and a core element of the band that gave the songs their distinct sound was gone. And it would be a while before a new lead guitarist was found.

Despite the internal upheaval, Fifth Angel had its major label recording contract. And the band was writing new songs. But before Epic gave Fifth Angel permission to record a new album, the label wanted to capitalize on the group's early buzz, and re-release Fifth Angel's debut. To do that, the label needed to negotiate with Mike Varney and Shrapnel Records.

Getting Fifth Angel out of their deal with Shrapnel and Roadrunner wasn't easy. It required a lot of negotiation behind the scenes to make it happen.

The parties came to an agreement that provided Varney with a percentage of sales from the eventual Epic re-release of *Fifth Angel*. Some in the media at the time questioned whether Fifth Angel hung Varney out to dry by moving to a major label. But Pilot didn't think so.

"What we gave him was more than fair for what he put into the band," Pilot said at the time. "We don't feel that we've screwed him at all. I don't know what he feels, but he hasn't expressed any dislike for the band or anything else; if he's really happy for us, he hasn't told us, but then he hasn't said he's mad at us either."

Once the legal hurdles were cleared, Epic's team went to work on *Fifth Angel* immediately. First up was reimagining the cover art. Art direction was handled by Stephen Byram, and the illustration of the brooding, intimidating angel on the new cover was provided by Amy Guip.

In addition to the new cover art, Fifth Angel anticipated making some changes to the songs on the album. Pilot told one writer at the time that he expected the tracks to be re-sequenced.

"What they're saying to us, in effect, is 'go ahead and finish it again,'" Pilot said at the time. "It's good to be able to put new ideas onto the songs—it's like being able to live with the album, let it grow, see what could be improved, and then improving it."

In what should be viewed as a testament to the quality of the original recording, the tracks were left completely alone. No changes were made to the music, aside from the songs being remastered. (The record was *not* remixed.) The media kit Epic Records issued for Fifth Angel described the band as "a gothic metal style act very much in the style of Iron Maiden. Serious lyrics with a sense of melody intertwined with screaming guitars and a heavy bottom end."

Epic Records' initial marketing plans for Fifth Angel's album were extensive. The label planned a media blitz on rock radio and print news outlets, extensive advertising and retail store promotions. Epic had their eyes on 13 key heavy metal magazines, particularly *Kerrang!* which had been staunch early supporters of the band. Approximately 70,000 clear, 7-inch flexi-discs were produced containing the song "Fifth Angel," and were attached to the February 1988 issue of the magazine.

There were other marketing ideas for *Fifth Angel* that were planned but did not come to fruition. For example, Epic was going to issue a 12-inch promotional white label vinyl record containing "In the Fallout" and "Fifth Angel"—the two tracks they were initially going to push from the album. But the record was never pressed. Similarly, stickers with the song name "In the Fallout" were also in the works for retail and hard rock radio giveaways that featured Fifth Angel's logo. Those, too, never saw the light of day.

But Fifth Angel was dedicated to the long run, so while some of the things promised to them never materialized, the group didn't take its deal with Epic lightly. The band was full-steam ahead and looking forward to a productive future.

"I look at being on a major label as a tool to put out better quality product and to get it promoted," Pilot said in a statement. "But it's still going to take the same amount of hard work and the same level of dedication on our part."

"I think there's a major gap in the market that we can fill," Mary added. "I really believe that our music's got a special quality, and that's something we want to keep on developing so that when kids go out and buy a Fifth Angel record, they know it's gonna be great."

One idea to boost Fifth Angel's profile was a music video for the album. According to Derek Simon, in early 1988, while Byrd was still in the band, Epic and Fifth Angel planned to shoot a video for "In the Fallout." A treatment was created for the music video, and a production crew was hired. It was going to be filmed in Los Angeles, and Simon flew to Los Angeles from New York to be with the band during the filming.

But at the eleventh hour, Simon was told the label was thinking about canceling the shoot. Executives at Columbia/Epic were going to meet the next morning to decide. With airline tickets already booked for Fifth Angel, and the band enroute to the airport, Simon elected, since there was a chance that the video was going to still happen, to have the group make the trip and not say anything to them.

The morning after Fifth Angel arrived in Los Angeles, Simon had to deliver the bad news that the video for "In the Fallout" had indeed been axed. Not surprisingly, the members of Fifth Angel were shocked that their video shoot was canceled. The band was angry, and while they weren't mad at Simon, the manager bore the brunt of the group's ire.

"I would have stopped them from coming if the decision was final," Simon said. "We thought we still had a puncher's chance. It was one of the most disappointing things that I've ever had to do in my professional life, telling the band that their video shoot was canceled."

It had been almost two years since Shrapnel Records had released *Fifth Angel*. But despite the time lapse, the band wasn't frustrated with Epic Records' insistence on reissuing the album. Pilot believed the promotional muscle of Epic would get the record a lot more exposure. And he was right.

Fifth Angel was reissued in March 1988. It hit the Billboard 200 chart for the first time on April 16, 1988, debuting at #188. It featured consecutive #1 most added weeks on metal radio, climbing to #2 on Hard Hitters,

FMQB's Metal Detector and CMJ Metal Charts.[17] Overall, *Fifth Angel* reached a peak position of #117 on June 11, 1988, and maintained a five-month run on the Billboard 200 chart.

Things were looking up for the band. But a lot of work was still needed for Fifth Angel to ascend to the heights they aspired to.

FOR WEEK ENDING JUNE 11, 1988

Billboard. TOP POP ALBUMS™ contin

THIS WEEK	LAST WEEK	2 WKS AGO	WKS. ON CHART	ARTIST — LABEL & NUMBER/DISTRIBUTING LABEL (SUG. LIST PRICE)*	TITLE
110	110	112	6	RIPPINGTONS FEATURING RUSS FREEMAN PASSPORT JAZZ PJ8042 (8.98) (CD)	KILIMANJARO
111	111	111	8	FATES WARNING METAL BLADE 73330/ENIGMA (8.98) (CD)	NO EXIT
112	113	101	12	BIG PIG A&M SP 6 5185 (6.98) (CD)	BONK
113	102	90	9	JESSE JOHNSON A&M SP 5188 (8.98) (CD)	EVERY SHADE OF LOVE
114	100	100	40	THE COVER GIRLS FEVER SFS 004/SUTRA (8.98) (CD)	SHOW ME
115	114	104	11	DAN REED NETWORK MERCURY 834 309 1/POLYGRAM (CD)	DAN REED NETWORK
116	103	86	13	SOUNDTRACK EMI-MANHATTAN 48680 (9.98) (CD)	SCHOOL DAZE
117	123	127	9	FIFTH ANGEL EPIC BFE 44201/E.P.A. (CD)	FIFTH ANGEL
118	137	151	4	REBA MCENTIRE MCA 42134 (8.98) (CD)	REBA
119	146	162	17	BASIA EPIC BFE 40767/E.P.A. (CD)	TIME AND TIDE
120	101	102	8	SUAVE CAPITOL C1-48686 (8.98) (CD)	I'M YOUR PLAYMATE
121	119	103	19	GEORGE THOROGOOD ● EMI-MANHATTAN 46973 (9.98) (CD)	BORN TO BE BAD

Fifth Angel's self-titled debut reached a peak of #117 on the Billboard 200 chart. Image courtesy of Ed Archer.

---

17. FMQB was *Friday Morning Quarterback*, a trade magazine that covered the radio and music industry at the time. CMJ was the *College Media Journal*, which focused on upcoming music and college music stations.

Ted Templeman
Senior Vice President

March 13, 1987

Ed Archer

RE: "Fifth Angel"

Dear Ed:

    I am returning the enclosed package to you. I have listened to the material along with the A & R Department and at this time, we have decided to pass.

    Thank you for thinking of me and Warner Bros. Records.

Sincerely,

Ted Templeman

TT/yg
enclosures

Warner Bros. Records/Reprise Records 3300 Warner Boulevard, Burbank, California 91510 (818) 846-9090

Before Fifth Angel connected with Derek Simon, the band shopped its album to a variety of major labels, only to be rejected. Warner Bros. was one of the labels that passed on Fifth Angel in 1987. Image courtesy of Ed Archer.

NIGHTSONG PRODUCTIONS

ROCK / METAL MUSIC PRODUCTION

ED ARCHER

P.O. BOX 40298
BELLEVUE, WA 98004
(206) 643-2733

TED PILOT

The business card Ed Archer and Ted Pilot used to promote Nightsong Productions. Image courtesy of Ed Archer.

An in-progress look at the new cover art for *Fifth Angel* on Epic Records. Image courtesy of Ed Archer.

The flexi-disc featuring "Fifth Angel" that was included with the February 27, 1988, issue of *Kerrang!* Also featured is an ad for the flexi-disc, and the cover of the issue it appeared with.

Fifth Angel's debut LP as released by Epic Records.

The promotional cassette of *Fifth Angel* issued by Epic Records.

L-R: James Byrd, John Macko, Ted Pilot, Ken Mary, Ed Archer

FIFTH ANGEL

Left to right: James Byrd -Lead guitar, John Macko -Bass, Ted Pilot -Vocals, Ed Archer -Rhythm guitar, Ken Mary -Drums

Photo by Joe Giron

Two promotional images of Fifth Angel used in 1987 and 1988.

⁘FIFTh ANGEL⁘

P.O. BOX 40298 -- BELLEVUE, WA 98004 -- USA

Greetings from FIFTH ANGEL!
And welcome to the fan club. We're going to do our best to bring you all the news and information, and keep you as up-to-date as possible on the band.

So much has been happening with FIFTH ANGEL lately. As most of you know, they have signed a deal with Epic Records. The first thing Epic did was to take the band's self-titled debut album and re-master it, so that the sound quality is about 100% better. They put it in a new package, and it's in the stores (and moving up the charts) now. It's also available on CD for the first time. If you have a copy of the original Shrapnel or Roadrunner LP, it's bound to be a collector's item very soon.

As far as the band's line-up goes, it's: TED PILOT on vocals, ED ARCHER and JAMES BYRD on guitars, new member JOHN MACKO on bass, and KEN K. MARY on drums. Yes, Ken is still a member of FIFTH ANGEL. In fact, he never left the band. Though he's recorded with the likes of Alice Cooper, Bonfire, David T. Chastain, and Giuffria, and completed two world tours drumming for Alice Cooper since the FIFTH ANGEL album was recorded, he is very much a member of this band, and this is where his energies will be focused from now on.

Watch for FIFTH ANGEL on tour this summer. We're expecting them to hit the road in June, and though it's been a long wait to get them on tour, it will have been worth it -- you won't be disappointed! After the tour, it'll be back into the studio to record a new album (the guys report that they have lots of material all ready to go).

The band will be shooting a video for the song "Fifth Angel" soon, so watch for it on MTV's Headbanger's Ball, and other video shows.

FIFTH ANGEL have been doing a lot of interviews, and their songs are getting some radio airplay, but we could definitely use your help in making others aware of the band! We hope you'll help to support them by calling radio stations and requesting your favorite FIFTH ANGEL songs, and by writing to magazines asking for more information on them. If you're interested in doing more to help out, please let us know!

Finally, we've made some changes in the fan club. My name is Mary Gail, and I'll be responsible for answering your mail, getting out the newsletters, etc. Though the guys do read each and every letter that comes in for them, they don't always have the time to personally answer everyone. So if you have any questions or comments, please send them to me, along with a self-addressed, stamped envelope (or an international reply coupon outside of the USA), and I will get back to you with an answer. I'd also like to work with you to make this fan club into what you want it to be. So let us know what you'd like to see in future newsletters, and tell us any suggestions you have to make it better.

Until next time, Keep Rockin'!

Mary Gail   May, 1988

A welcome letter from Mary Gail of the Fifth Angel fan club in May 1988.

In His Words

Ed Archer on Building the Guitar He Used on Fifth Angel's First Album

It was the early 1980s, and I remember going to Boogie Bodies in Puyallup, Washington, driving about two hours from where I lived. Boogie Bodies was a very small company created by Lynn Ellsworth who worked together with Wayne Charvel. That's how Eddie Van Halen got the parts for his famous Frankenstein guitar! The [company's] "showroom" was actually the living room of Lynn's house. There were guitar necks and bodies everywhere!

Anyway, I got a good deal on the neck because it had a defect (small hairline crack near the nut). I mounted the neck onto a DiMarzio body made of ash wood. I'd ordered most of the guitar parts from a place called The Music Emporium—Schaller tuners, DiMarzio body, volume pot and such. I was friends with Floyd Rose back then, so I got the locking tremolo directly from him, and I was a huge fan of Eddie Van Halen (still am) so I installed a Seymour Duncan Custom pickup!

The original look of the guitar was different from what you see now. It was a natural finish without a pick guard. I had James Byrd paint it black for me and I added the chrome pick guard. It still plays and sounds great! Whenever I play it, I'm reminded of the time and effort it took to put it together, especially scalloping the fretboard. We didn't have a bass player at that time, so I recorded the bass tracks using a borrowed Yamaha bass. But that's another story.

Boogie Bodies

We've been building the finest necks for over 3 years. Thousands of players world-wide know our feel and playing ease. We think you, too, should know why Boogie Bodies necks are the finest available.

- Finest hard maple, rosewood and ebony
- Jumbo frets, not too big - not too small
- 10" radius fingerboard, for playing ease
- Popular small peghead
- Laminated fingerboard for strength & stability
- Double expanding truss rod for quick sure adjustment
- Comfortable feeling contoured back. V shape also available
- Available in 2 widths, 1 11/16 or 1 3/4 at the nut
- Available at any stage of completion for those wishing to customize their own neck
- We don't make them fast, we make them right.

Ask for us at your favorite dealers
for more information Send 50¢ to
**BOOGIE BODIES, P.O. Box 1244
Puyallup, WA 98371   (206) 848-3752**

Pictured in the middle is the Strat-style guitar Ed Archer built and used to record all the rhythm guitar tracks on *Fifth Angel*. It remains one of his favorite guitars.

Photo by and courtesy of Ed Archer/Fifth Angel.

> "You know how slim your chance is, trapped here alive."
>
> - Fifth Angel, "Only the Strong Survive"

Chapter 4
Only the Strong Survive

Fifth Angel spent much of 1988 promoting their first record, rehearsing songs for potential tours, and writing for their next album. The band's lineup was in flux, however, as they were still without a lead guitarist, and Ken Mary was busy touring with Alice Cooper, and later, House of Lords.

The drummer was very much an in-demand player at this point, both in the studio and on the road. In addition to the two TKO records Mary was a part of (1984's *In Your Face*, and 1985's *Below the Belt*), he had recorded three albums with Chastain (*Ruler of the Wasteland*, *The 7th of Never*, and *The Voice of the Cult*), the 1988 self-titled debut of House of Lords, and appears on Alice Cooper's 1987 record, *Raise Your Fist and Yell*.

Mary's connection with Cooper began at the Whisky a Go Go on Sunset Boulevard in West Hollywood, California. It was 1986, and the drummer was touring with his old friend, Randy Hansen. Alice Cooper's management was in the audience that night and invited him to audition for the shock rocker's new band. Mary finished the tour, flew home, and then spent his own money (which was quite a lot in the mid-1980s) to fly back down to Los Angeles to audition. He got the spot and was with Alice Cooper for two years. Ken also appears on the live recording, *The Nightmare Returns*, which was recorded on October 31, 1986, and released in 1987.

Despite his busy schedule, Mary was still very much an active member of Fifth Angel. Ken used his time on the road and in the spotlight to help promote the band.

"I would go meet with *Kerrang!* and *Metal Hammer*—all these publications that were very important in that day," Mary said. "Had I not been there, would we have gotten those interviews and placements in the magazines? I don't know. It helped. Initially it helped.

"Honestly, it was a dual-edge sword," Mary added. "In some ways, it helped quite a bit because I do think we definitely had attention, and we had a lot of press that we may not have gotten otherwise. At the same time, being on tour with Alice did keep Fifth Angel from touring."

Fifth Angel did have some touring opportunities presented to them, however. According to Pilot, Fifth Angel was considered for an opening slot on the U.S. leg of Ozzy Osbourne's 1988-1989 tour supporting *No Rest for the Wicked*. Fifth Angel attended an Epic Records party in March 1988 in Los Angeles, where they met Ozzy's band. Pilot and Zakk Wylde, Ozzy's guitarist, even posed for a picture together. Unfortunately, Fifth Angel didn't get the tour, losing out to a combination of bands that included Anthrax, White Lion, and Vixen.

"I do recall getting excited about it, because everything else up to that point had really fallen into place, as far as climbing the ladder of achievement," Archer said. "It was a continuation of the excitement when we started discussing going on tour in support of a big-name act."

There were some other offers to open for established headliners (Macko and Archer both recall the band being considered as a support act for the Scorpions), but nothing panned out. Fifth Angel made the effort to be ready, however, honing its live show throughout 1988. Macko said he believed the show would come together real fast and easy, and thought "In the Fallout" would be one song that would go over well live with fans.

Pilot was keen to hit the stage as well.

"We just want to out there right from the start, have the show really kick some ass, and have it sound great," the singer said.

Regretfully, presenting Fifth Angel live was not in the cards at the time. To this day, Macko was adamant that Fifth Angel made a colossal mistake by not hitting the road in support of its debut album, especially once they were signed to Epic.

"I was just expecting us to go on tour, why wouldn't we go on tour?" Macko said. "I still just can't believe how we didn't go and tour for that first album and how that fell through the cracks."

"I love to play live. There's not better feeling in the world than singing to a large group of people," Pilot added. "That's one reason it was so disappointing."

Fifth Angel made the most of its time, however. The band was extremely prolific with its songwriting. The first three songs they came up with for their second record were "Cathedral," "We Rule," and a ballad, "Broken Dreams." The tracks showcased the band's growth, but also retained "a raw metal edge" from their first album that Fifth Angel believed had earned them the respect of European fans.

Ken Mary was enthusiastic about Fifth Angel's direction when asked about a new album in 1988.

"The new songs are incredible! It'll definitely be a step above the last one," Mary said. "There's a progression in the new material, a versatility that maybe didn't show as much before. We've learned how to get the sound we want, our own sound. That's taken us three years to achieve but it will definitely be Fifth Angel!"

Fifth Angel also needed a new lead guitarist who could handle the heralded guitar solos James Byrd recorded on their first record, and bring something new to the table. And they found a great one—a local prodigy named Kendall Bechtel.

Kendall Bechtel was born in December 1966. He was exposed at an early age to bands such as The Beatles, The Rolling Stones, Jimi Hendrix, Santana, Credence Clearwater Revival, Deep Purple, and Led Zeppelin. Bechtel picked up the guitar at age five, playing around with it sporadically until he got serious a few years later.

Kendall took lessons, learning from a variety of teachers that immersed him in the styles of folk and rock. After learning chords, scales, and some theory, Kendall was able, with the help of his parents, to buy a Memphis Les Paul, a Fender Champ amplifier, and a Big Muff fuzz pedal. The allure of rock and roll grabbed him, and he spent hours absorbing the nuances of artists such as Peter Frampton, and of course, the "heavy metal" of the day in the form of Van Halen, KISS, Scorpions, UFO, Judas Priest, Black Sabbath, Rush, and more.

As his skill level grew, Kendall performed sporadically,

even as an elementary school student. He formed and joined several school bands, before hooking up with an outfit called Rage in junior high school. Around 1982, he took some lessons from local Seattle guitarist (and future record producer) Kelly Gray, who loaned Kendall a black Gibson Flying V guitar for a high school talent show performance of "Hell Bent for Leather" by Judas Priest.

During his high school years, Bechtel was in a few bands, playing mostly covers of Judas Priest, UFO and Rainbow. For a short time, he was in a band called Fallen Angel with Davey French from Everclear. Bechtel also lived at Gray's house for about six months. Gray's mother, Marie, was a local music teacher, and Kendall joined a band with Kelly's brother, David (Dee) Howard Gray, called Steel Sea (later named The Heat), and the group recorded a four-song demo.

Over the next several years, Kendall kept playing music, working odd jobs until he found out about the audition for Fifth Angel. According to Bechtel, the guy who tipped him off to Fifth Angel was the same person who did so with John Macko—Richard Gibson of Myth. But there are conflicting stories. Macko remembers Kelly Gray being the one who recommended Bechtel, and Tim Branom recalls mentioning Kendall to the band, but regardless, the introduction was made. As Kendall tells it, it was John who did the preliminary check on him, and the bassist came away impressed and invited Bechtel to officially audition.

"I drove all the way out to Duvall, where Kendall was living and sat down in his bedroom and he played for me," Macko said. "I was blown away. I was like, 'Fuck, this guy is amazing.' I left a tape and said, 'Hey, learn these songs.' Then I reported back to Ted and Ed and said, 'This guy's really good. We need to check him out.'"

An audition was scheduled, and Kendall plugged in and jammed.

"I was a little nervous and remember not doing so well on the first album's material," Bechtel said. "But, when they started playing the [new] songs, it allowed me to play some leads off the cuff and they were impressed."

Kendall cut a demo of the new songs with the band, which impressed representatives with Epic Records. Still, it took several rehearsals and about three months of work before Bechtel got the call that the job was his.

Pilot explained that once word got around that Fifth Angel needed a new lead guitarist, tapes from prospective players came in from all over the world. The singer called it "audition hell," but Kendall was clearly the choice.

"We wanted someone who could play rippingly fast, but also slow down," Pilot said at the time. "Most of the guys who auditioned tried to impress us with blazing licks. But we wanted someone who'd fit the band's melodic style of playing, and someone we'd get along with."

"When they finally told me I got the gig, we all went out to dinner and celebrated," Bechtel added. "We couldn't wait to get into the studio to do the album."

On a side note, when this author visited both Bechtel and Byrd in October 2006, the guitarists told the story about the first time they met. Once Bechtel got the job with Fifth Angel, he stopped by a local studio to see Byrd (who was recording a solo record at the time), hoping the band's former guitarist would give him some pointers about the guitar solos on *Fifth Angel*. Byrd said he told Bechtel, "If you knew the story behind my leaving, you wouldn't have asked." Byrd then relayed his side of the story behind his dismissal to Bechtel. Through that encounter, the two guitarists struck up a friendship, which eventually led to a future musical collaboration. (Which will be discussed in the pages ahead.)

The initial plan for a second Fifth Angel album was for the band to hit the studio in August 1988. That didn't happen. And then the band members started to notice that Epic wasn't promoting Fifth Angel as much as they had initially promised them. All that influence and money at a major label's disposal, and Fifth Angel didn't get on a tour, nor did they really receive significantly more press.

The lack of support from Epic Records was a source of great disappointment for everyone in the band. Ken Mary explained that while he has nothing but respect for Epic, at the time, they really didn't have any heavy metal bands of Fifth Angel's style on the roster. As a result, he felt that Epic probably wasn't sure what to do with the band.

"For instance, let's say you have Def Leppard on your label, and Def Leppard is blowing up, and they're huge. Then you have this new band, Fifth Angel. What you can do is leverage Fifth Angel with Def Leppard," Ken said. "You can say, 'Hey, Def Leppard is coming into town next month. If you stock Fifth Angel albums, we'll give you 20 extra tickets and 20 extra backstage passes.' You can do that with radio stations. You use the muscle of your major artists to basically elevate your new artists. Epic had nothing really to work with in that regard."

To be fair, Epic did have New York rockers Living Colour, who released *Vivid* (featuring the hit singles "Cult of Personality", "Glamour Boys", and "Open Letter (To a Landlord)") in May 1988. In fact, Archer remembers getting an advance copy of *Vivid* from Bruce Calder, an engineer at Steve Lawson Productions who had moved to New York to continue his record producing career. Archer and Pilot were researching potential studios to record *Time Will Tell*, and asked Calder if he had any recommendations on where to record drums.

"I remember we were over at Ted's dad's house, and we pop the cassette in the stereo, and Ted and I just looked at each other and our fucking jaws dropped," Archer said. "We're like, 'holy shit, listen to these drums! This is awesome!'"[18]

Epic also landed another Seattle metal band, Sanctuary, whose debut, *Refuge Denied*, was engineered by Terry Date. The album was recorded at Steve Lawson Productions and released in 1988. Sanctuary's follow-up, *Into the Mirror Black*, was also recorded at Steve Lawson Productions and produced by Howard Benson.

In fact, Fifth Angel and Sanctuary were often joined at the hip during the late-1980s and early-1990s. The two bands were paired on a promotional LP titled *Interchords - Words and Music* in 1988. In addition, both groups appeared on *Megahurtz*, a 12-inch vinyl, CD, and cassette promotional release that also featured Riot V and Slammin' Watusis. Fifth Angel's "In the Fallout" and "Call Out the Warning" led off the record. Despite the early positive buzz for Fifth Angel, not everyone was impressed with the band, however. In reviewing the compilation for *Kerrang!* Howard

---

18. Calder didn't work on *Vivid*, and Fifth Angel didn't record at any of the studios where *Vivid* was recorded. But Pilot and Archer's reaction certainly reinforced that Fifth Angel was on a label capable of producing great hard rock and metal.

Johnson called Fifth Angel "flat and insignificant as the dregs of yesterday's lager frenzy."

"The band go for the grandiose with 'In the Fallout' and 'Call Out the Warning,' but end up strictly small-town," Johnson added.[19]

Aside from the compilation album appearances, a couple of interviews and a few random magazine ads, the attention paid to Fifth Angel was minimal. After years of waiting for their big breakthrough, Ken Mary felt Epic simply wasn't investing enough time or money in Fifth Angel. And Ken did not want Fifth Angel to get lumped in with bands he felt weren't quite the same stylistically. So, instead of making grand demands, Ken stepped out of Fifth Angel to forge his own path.

Ken's stint with Alice Cooper was over, but he joined House of Lords, a melodic hard rock band featuring keyboardist Gregg Giuffria. It was an opportunity to record with engineer/producer Andy Johns (Led Zeppelin, The Rolling Stones, etc.) and get on the road. Ken felt bad, but he had let other opportunities to advance his career go by due to his loyalty to Fifth Angel. And he had to start thinking about the future.

"I talked to the guys in the band about it and said, 'Look, they're not spending any money on our promotion,'" Mary said of Epic Records. "I looked at it and went, 'These guys are doing nothing for us. I don't want to waste my life doing this.' … That's why I left. Epic was just tossing us out there.

---

19. Fifth Angel wasn't the only target of Johnson's ire. He criticized all the bands on *Megahurtz*, calling them "four American little leaguers" and questioned what the point of the sampler album was.

"Every band that doesn't succeed blames their label," the drummer added. "In this case, I think it is accurate because if they thought something was there, they could have put some of that Michael Jackson money into us. You look at that and you go, 'Did they have the money? Did they have the power? Could they have put the pedal down a little bit more on the band?' Yes. Apparently, they didn't see what we saw in ourselves."

Fifth Angel soldiered on without Ken Mary, continuing to write songs for their next record. As the calendar turned to 1989, the band was ready to record. But now they needed to find a new drummer. And it wasn't going to be an easy process.

Derek Simon lined up several drummers for Fifth Angel to audition as the band approached going into the studio. One of them was Mikkey Dee. The Swedish drummer was fresh off working with King Diamond, having recorded *Fatal Portrait* (1986), *Abigail* (1987) and *Them* (1988).

Dee didn't work out, but it wasn't because of his playing ability. On that front, Fifth Angel was blown away.

"Derek flew Mikkey up to Seattle and we played with Mikkey, and, of course, he was amazing," Macko said. "He just wanted too much money. He and I became buddies for a while."

Fifth Angel also auditioned John Tempesta for its vacant drummer position. Eventually, Tempesta would make a name for himself with Exodus, Testament, White Zombie, Rob Zombie, and The Cult. But in 1989, he was just finishing work as a drum tech for Anthrax's Charlie Benante. According to Macko, Tempesta, at least at the time, wasn't at the performance level that Fifth Angel felt they needed from a drummer.

"To be honest, he wasn't great then," Macko said, laughing. "He was okay, but compared to Ken Mary, we just didn't feel he was strong enough. Tempesta had the last laugh though!"

With numerous drummer auditions and no viable candidates, time was running short. Fifth Angel had come up with an album's worth of new songs, studio time to record was booked, and the clock was ticking. Simon sent one more drummer to the band for an audition, Joey Pafumi, who was recommended by Paul Stanley of KISS. Pafumi was living in Los Angeles at the time, but was originally from Beverly, Massachusetts.

Pafumi, who had recently left the hard rock band XYZ, flew to Seattle to rehearse with Fifth Angel. The drummer did two weeks of pre-production with the band, but not everyone was convinced Pafumi was the right guy for the job. Macko said he felt Pafumi was "off," and had reservations about committing to him.

"I'm like, 'He's not good,'" Macko said. "But we didn't really have anybody else and it was getting down to the wire."

Pilot and Archer thought Pafumi was good enough to play on the record, however. Archer said he recalled Pafumi making some errors, yet the guitarist felt the situation would work itself out. Pafumi got the gig, and Fifth Angel was a full band again and ready to record their second album. But while the quintet was looking forward to its trip to New York City to start tracking new songs, more drama was right around the corner.

From left to right: John Macko, Ted Pilot, Sean McNabb, Hanna Bolte, and Ken Mary at an Epic Records party in March 1988. Photo courtesy of John Macko.

Zakk Wylde and Ted Pilot at an Epic Records party in March 1988. Photo courtesy of Ted Pilot.

A promotional photo of Fifth Angel issued by Epic Records in late-1988/early-1989. From left to right: Ed Archer, Kendall Bechtel, Ted Pilot, John Macko. Photo courtesy of John Macko.

The promotional releases that Fifth Angel appeared on in 1988.

In His Words

John Macko's Spinal Tap Moment While Recording Time Will Tell

We were doing drum tracks and some other basic stuff at Mediasound Studios in Manhattan. The band was running through some of the songs in the studio's main live room where the drums were set up for recording, Ed and Kendall both had Marshall stacks, and I had a Bi-amped bass rig (old school) that was provided by the studio.

 Due to the extremely loud volume at which we were playing, I was getting drowned out by the guitar amps quickly, so I had to crank that bass amp up, well after a short while I started to smell a burning scent that appeared to be coming from the bass rig. Upon inspection of the amp, I didn't see or smell anything from it, so I ignored it and turned it up some more and kept playing! A few minutes later I smelled it again and turned around and looked at the rig and smoke is pouring out of the single 18" Sunn cabinet which then burst into flames! Yeah, the fucking speaker cabinet caught on fire!

 Our record producer Terry Brown rushes into the room with a fire extinguisher and puts the fire out! And here is the photo of the aftermath! I will never forget this story as long as I live!

The remains of John Macko's speaker cabinet that caught fire during the *Time Will Tell* recording sessions.

Photo courtesy of John Macko/Fifth Angel.

*All alone in a change,
may be a lonely place.
Everything is so strange,
in this race..."*

Fifth Angel, "Time Will Tell"

Chapter 5
Time Will Tell

Fifth Angel spent almost two years writing and refining the songs for their next album. In fall 1988, Epic finally gave the band a green light to move forward with the recording process. This galvanized the group, and spirits were high that Fifth Angel was headed in the right direction.

Pilot believed the band's new material had what it took to make it big and propel Fifth Angel to new heights. But he, like the recently departed Ken Mary, knew success was going to come down to the almighty dollar.

"I hope Epic gets behind us all the way," Pilot said at the time. "So much depends on marketing these days. Some of the bands who've made it big lately—I won't name names—are so untalented. With the right promotion you can turn a half-assed band into superstars. We're so much better than a lot of the bands who've made it."

At first, Fifth Angel planned to repeat the same recording process they used with their debut album. They wanted Terry Date to engineer and for Fifth Angel to self-produce the record with his help. But Date wasn't available, and Epic wanted a bigger name producer. Two names surfaced: Max Norman and Terry Brown.

Norman produced and/or engineered Ozzy Osbourne's

first few solo albums. *Blizzard of Ozz* (1980), *Diary of a Madman* (1981), and *Bark at the Moon* (1983) were all immensely successful and put Ozzy on the map as a solo artist. In addition, Norman's work with Y&T on *Black Tiger* (1982), Loudness on *Thunder in the East* (1985) and Savatage on *Power of the Night* (1985) stood out. Norman seemed a natural fit to produce Fifth Angel at the time.

Brown, the acclaimed producer of Rush from the band's inception through 1982's *Signals*, was widely praised by Fifth Angel. Brown was also coming off a smash pop hit with "(I Just) Died in Your Arms" by Cutting Crew, which appears on the group's 1986 debut, *Broadcast*. Archer and Pilot had played Rush tunes for years while in Ridge, and they loved the Canadian power trio, so it seemed like Terry Brown was a good fit as well.

"I know Max Norman was discussed," Simon said. "Max had produced the third Grim Reaper record, *Rock You to Hell*, and obviously we had a relationship with Terry Date from Fifth Angel's first record, but he also worked with Metal Church, and he was getting a lot of work in those days. I feel like it was just simply a scheduling thing. I don't remember anybody other than those three people expressing interest, or that we sought out."

Archer remembers that with Date not an option, the band chose Norman initially, due to his hard rock and metal pedigree. But while Fifth Angel was still debating, Norman accepted a different project, and Simon said Fifth Angel would have needed to wait another six months to record. The band and the label did not want to wait. So, Terry Brown ended up being the choice.

Not everyone in the band was thrilled with losing some of their creative control, however. But on a major label, Fifth Angel learned that's the way it goes.

"Terry [Brown] did a good job, but of course, Epic told us pretty much that we were going to use him," Pilot confirmed. "He had a really different personality and specific ways he did things. What had worked for him in the past, he did again. It was definitely a different way to record."

"I don't really have a problem with Terry Brown's production on that record," Simon said of *Time Will Tell*. "Everybody brings a different skill set to the table. Terry was a song guy, but maybe he wasn't a song guy in the same way Max Norman was a song guy. All of Terry's records sound great. But maybe Max makes a record or turns a song into something better. I don't really recall Terry screwing with the songs very much, in terms of what the band brought to the table. And maybe that would have helped, maybe it wouldn't have helped, who knows? Hindsight is certainly 20/20. The combination of comfort with Terry Brown and the schedule was how the decision was made."

Preproduction for the album took place in the Pacific Northwest. Archer's employer had a large warehouse, and his boss let the band store their gear there and use the space to rehearse. Brown flew into Seattle to take part in the process, and once preproduction was completed, the project shifted to New York so the band could begin recording.

Fifth Angel entered Mediasound to record the bed tracks for their new album in early 1989. The recording studio was originally a Baptist church, located at 311 West 57th Street in New York City. Bands such as Aerosmith and The Rolling Stones recorded there, and *Appetite for Destruction* by Guns N' Roses was mixed at the studio as well. For Fifth Angel, first up at the legendary facility was tracking the drums, and the band's worst fear was quickly realized: Pafumi wasn't going to work out. Recording at

Mediasound wasn't cheap, and decisions needed to be made in short order.

Macko remembered being on the studio floor with Pafumi on the first day of tracking, trying to guide the drummer through one song, and Joey just wasn't up to the challenge at the time. The band discussed it and gave Pafumi one more day to get things sorted out, but it just didn't come together.

Luckily for Fifth Angel, an old friend had a few free days and flew into New York to help his buddies out. Ken Mary saved the day. The drummer had a small break in his touring schedule. Simon arranged it so Ken could fly in and cut all 11 new Fifth Angel songs over a span of less than two days.

For Ken, it was like old times making music with his former bandmates. For Simon, the band, and the label, Ken Mary was a Godsend to be able to track drums on such short notice.

"It was like, 'Ken's going to bail us out here,'" Simon said. "If Ken wasn't available, you get into a situation of whoever comes in next needs to nail these parts. I must have had such relief that Ken worked it out to be there. I would have flown him in from Antarctica if I had to."

Ken said he used the drum kit of KISS drummer Eric Carr on the recording, which he found profoundly cool. (Derek Simon, however, doesn't recall that being the case, but Pafumi confirmed that Carr had loaned him the drum kit to record the album.) On top of that thrill, Ken, being a self-proclaimed "Neil Peart freak," was excited to work with Terry Brown and hear the producer's stories about Rush. Thankfully, since Ken had been on the demos of some of the new Fifth Angel songs, the material was generally familiar, which helped him knock the recording out of the park.

"We grew up together, worked hard to make this thing

happen and see it through," Mary said. "It was just stepping in as a session drummer, but a different feeling, because these are guys who I knew," Mary said. "I had a lot of fun, I really enjoyed it, and the guys did too. They were happy to just move forward."

Pilot was thrilled that Ken was able to join them. The three of them (including Archer) had been friends since they were kids and having them all together in New York just felt "right" to the singer.

"Ken was a really good friend of mine, and we spent a lot of personal time just hanging out," Pilot said. "It was a bummer [when he left the band], and we didn't want to do the album without him, initially. ... He just picked it up really quickly and it was easy for him."

Macko's bass tracks were also cut at Mediasound. He used just two bass guitars (neither of which he owned at the time) to record the songs on *Time Will Tell*. One was a Warwick RockBass Streamer, and the other was a Steinberger XM-2 bass.

"I used the Streamer on most of the tracks, and I fell in love with it right away; deep rich tone and solid as a rock," Macko said. "You can really hear that tone during the verses on 'So Long.' The Steinberger on the other hand had quite a different tone which you can hear on 'Angel of Mercy' and a few other songs."

Although it was a hectic week in the studio, Fifth Angel did have fun. The band went out sightseeing, visiting the World Trade Center, going out to pubs with Terry Brown and Max Norman (who ironically was in the building working on another album) and hearing their stories about working with various bands.

On a humorous note, Archer even got a little starstruck while waiting to enter Mediasound one day.

"I remember waiting to get buzzed in, and here comes Little Steven from Bruce Springsteen's E Street Band," Archer said. "So here he is, and we're waiting and I'm wondering what to say and do. I froze up and never said anything. That's one of my regrets. I should have reached out and been a little more outgoing just for the experience, if nothing else. It would have made a lot of sense for me to step out of my shell and do some networking."

Fifth Angel attended the rehearsal of KISS vocalist/guitarist Paul Stanley, who was preparing for a solo tour at the time. Archer recalled that he and Bechtel were too starstruck to introduce themselves. Instead of making small talk with the KISS frontman, Archer said he simply asked if Stanley had seen manager Derek Simon. When Stanley said "no," the two Fifth Angel members quickly excited the room.

Pilot and Macko also visited KISS' warehouse in Manhattan, where they checked out the band's gear. While Fifth Angel weren't necessarily huge KISS fans, the hookup to check everything out was arranged by their manager, Derek Simon, who was working with KISS at the time.

Some of it was even captured on video by Ted Pilot, who brought along a video camcorder to document Fifth Angel's experiences.

"In the hotel room, there were these KISS dolls, and Ted would make this thing where he would zoom in on the dolls and be like, 'Hey, Gene, what do you think about this,'" Macko said. "We just did all kinds of crazy stuff. We had a lot of fun."

After the drums and bass guitar tracks were cut, Fifth Angel relocated to Carriage House Studios, in Stamford, Connecticut, to record the balance of the album. The Seattleites got their taste of late winter in New England, as

Macko recalls he and Pilot going out for jogs in the snow. The band lived at Carriage House during the recording, as there were apartments above the control room.

Fifth Angel bonded with Brown during their time together, and everyone enjoyed the experience.

"Terry was very warm and personable and became a father figure to us because of his experience, so I'd just refer to him as 'Father Brown,'" Bechtel said.

"He was a real kick to work with and a lot of fun as far as I was concerned," Macko added, regarding Brown. "He would always have a smile on his face, a Heineken in his hand and was always making jokes."

As discussed earlier, Archer and Pilot had a distinct, somewhat monotonous way they recorded the latter's lead vocals. The pair went line by line with lots of punch-ins to ensure the raw cut was perfect. But Brown, according to Pilot, wanted to record vocals with a lot of effects on them from the jump. They tried doing it Brown's way at first, but after an unsuccessful session, the producer relented, and Archer and Pilot went back to their method.

"I remember vividly, we started tracking the vocals, and Ted and I were well established about how we did it, and we were nervous working under a big-time producer," Archer said. "Ted was the one who brought it up to Terry Brown, and Terry's like, 'That's not how I do it.' I had this sinking feeling about it, and I think Ted had the same feeling. They spent a couple of hours working on it and I don't know if it was that evening or the next day, but Terry said, 'You know what, you guys have a rapport, go ahead and do it the way you want to do it.' So, I did it the same way on the second record like I did on the first record, being Ted's ears and critic. Hat's off to Terry for being so cool and flexible with us. There's probably a lot of producers who wouldn't have given a shit and would have recorded it the way they wanted to. Terry trusted us to get it right."

Fifth Angel spent a lot of their studio time at the Carriage House recording rhythm guitars and vocals, which also put Bechtel behind the eight-ball for his lead guitar lines. That worked out just the way he liked it, according to the guitarist.

"On the song 'Wait for Me,' I had 20 minutes to come up with something before tracking it, so that was kind of challenging," Bechtel said. "Most of the solos were basically improvisational. I like that, because it gives a lively feeling to them."

One of the more guitar-centered tracks on the album is Fifth Angel's cover of "Lights Out" by UFO. Pilot said the band had wanted to record a cover song for a long time and were listening to *Strangers in the Night* prior to hitting the studio. They all dug UFO's performance of the iconic "Lights Out," and quickly decided that was the one they wanted to record for their album. Fifth Angel made some minor adjustments to the song structure, and then basically handed the track off to Kendall. That was right up Bechtel's alley.

"Schenker's in my blood," Bechtel said, referring to Michael Schenker, the lead guitarist on UFO's "Lights Out." "I didn't want to change his solo around too much. I don't think I sound like him too much on the rest of the album."

Once they were out of time at Carriage House, Fifth Angel went home to finish the recording. Background vocals and keyboards were done at Triad Studios, in Redmond, Washington. It was at Triad where Fifth Angel experimented with someone other than Pilot laying down some vocal lines. On "Seven Hours," the astute listener will hear a second voice whisper "seven, hours" during the chorus. That's Archer, who thought the whispers would add a more dynamic element to the song.

Fifth Angel finished up in short order at Triad Studios. At that point, Brown took the recordings to Metalworks Studios in Mississauga, Ontario, Canada, to mix the album. His mix engineer was Noel Golden, with Stuart Young serving as a recording assistant. Canadian singer-songwriter Lisa Dal Bello also recorded some backing vocals for the tracks "Broken Dreams" and "So Long" at Metalworx. *Time Will Tell* was mastered, submitted to Epic Records, and preparations were made to release Fifth Angel's long-awaited second LP.

Released on August 23, 1989, *Time Will Tell* was a bit of a departure for fans of Fifth Angel's first album. While the new record had its share of heavy hitters, such as "We Rule," it was much more melodic, having more in common with acts like the Scorpions and Europe. Pilot agreed with the similarities, saying at the time that those bands were known for their powerful melodic songs, and so was Fifth Angel.

Pilot was even more forward about Fifth Angel's evolution in Epic Records' official press release about *Time Will Tell*. The singer tried to somewhat distance the band from its metal roots to appeal to a broader demographic.

"We liked the first album, and it was well received, but we had to make the album a heavier album than we originally intended," Pilot said. "At that time, Shrapnel Records was catering to an underground scene, so we came up with this intensely Gothic-sounding record. *Time Will Tell* is much more like the album we always wanted to make. This is the true Fifth Angel."

In various interviews from 1989, Pilot asserted that

some of Fifth Angel's more AOR-oriented material wasn't permitted to be on the band's first album by Shrapnel Records President Mike Varney. Varney, not surprisingly, disagreed wholeheartedly with that statement.

"That's not a fair assessment of the situation. I just wanted the album to appeal to Shrapnel's audience—guitar-oriented and, for the most part, fairly heavy rock," Varney said. "From the day I signed Fifth Angel, the band knew my label was aimed at an underground, street-level following, and that I wasn't going to turn out any hits. I just wanted a great metal band, not something geared to AM radio. My audience doesn't want the commercial stuff."

Objectively, *Time Will Tell* does a good job balancing musical styles between where Fifth Angel was and what they wanted to be at the time. "Cathedral," the album's lead track, is a perfect example, blending the aggression and references to religious diction and symbolism with a more defined melodic touch. Indeed, the entirety of *Time Will Tell* feels like a natural progression from the songs "Fifth Angel," "Wings of Destiny" and "Shout it Out" from the band's first record.

Edgar Klüsener, writing for *Metal Hammer*, called Fifth Angel's debut a "prime specimen of goth rock, partly mystical, even bombastic, obviously influenced by the Dio school of rock," while he felt *Time Will Tell* focused on a more "straightforward rock" direction.

"In 1989 Fifth Angel are mainly concerned with classic rock 'n' roll themes, with the yearnings and desires of our generation, with heroes and broken dreams, small catastrophes and great passions," Klüsener wrote.

Reflecting on *Time Will Tell* in 2025, Pilot called the album a more "mature" Fifth Angel, noting that the band got the more melodic sound it was looking for, along with a continuity amongst the 11 tracks.

"*Time Will Tell*, from my standpoint, was actually about making major changes in your life and going different directions because life is difficult and lonely," Pilot said. "That's what it was really about. It was about me. It wasn't about relationships directly, it was … about changing your direction in life, and the only person that could do that is yourself."

Musically, the members of Fifth Angel all agree that *Time Will Tell* was a push by the band to get a more mainstream sound. It is still grounded in European power metal, but Bechtel perhaps summed it up best when he said the album "was trying to be more commercially palatable."

Macko praised the record, however, noting his favorite tracks are the two ballads, "Broken Dreams" and "So Long." The bassist added that he really likes all the songs on *Time Will Tell*, except for "Feel the Heat," which he felt wasn't quite up to the quality of the other 10 tracks. Macko co-wrote "Wait for Me," which marked his songwriting debut with the band. (The track was co-written with Archer and Pilot.)

Archer loves the heavier and more epic songs on *Time Will Tell*, namely "We Rule" and the album opener, "Cathedral." "Seven Hours" is another tune Archer is still quite fond of today, heaping praise on Pilot's abilities as a songwriter and singer to make that song shine.

"Ted was really good at coming up with melodies and phrasing that would be like a point-counterpoint with the guitars and other instrumentation," Archer said. "On 'Seven Hours,' just thinking of the verses and the phrasing and how it goes relative to the guitars, I really like that one."

In short, *Time Will Tell* had a sound and sheen fit for the time. In addition, Epic Records authorized a music video for the title track. Produced by Giuliana Schnitzler and directed by Steve Goldmann, the video for "Time Will Tell" was shot in an old desanctified place of worship in New York and received some initial airplay on MTV in late 1989 and early 1990. Because the building had no power, a truck with a massive generator was brought in to provide power for the lighting. Two cameras were used, including a boom crane on tracks. The footage was captured on 16mm film.

Archer remembers it being a long day of filming, but one filled with laughs, both with the young people who were hired as extras, and his bandmates. But what he recalls most vividly were his...boots.

"I had this particular pair of snakeskin cowboy boots," Archer said. "We're changing to go shoot the video, and Kendall sees me wearing these boots and he really likes them. And he says, 'Hey Ed, do you think I can wear your cowboy boots, I really dig those, they'd really match what I'm doing.' Me, being the nice guy I sometimes am, I said, 'I guess so.' So, here are these cool looking boots that I was going to wear for the video, and Kendall wore them. I wore his, and it turns out his foot size is a little smaller, and halfway through the video shoot, my feet are fucking killing me, because I'm wearing Kendall's boots, not mine."

Bechtel co-wrote "Time Will Tell" with Archer and Pilot. The mid-tempo cut has a powerful and melodic chorus which likely influenced its choice as the album's lead single. But the solo is a 28-second energetic and melodic frenzy that showcases the skill of Fifth Angel's new lead guitarist.

The video for "Time Will Tell" also featured a new drummer for the band, Richard Stuverud. Fifth Angel auditioned him and a few others throughout the spring and summer of 1989, after the band returned home from recording the new album.

Stuverud cut his teeth touring with The Fastbacks, a punk rock band from Seattle. Stuverud was fresh off recording an EP with Suicide Squad, a group comprised of himself, vocalist Brad Sinsel and guitarist Rick Pierce of TKO, and bassist Rick Bradley. The EP, *Live it While You Can*, came out in 1988, and was released by Music for Nations in Europe.

Shortly afterward, Stuverud formed War Babies with his friend, guitarist Tommy "Gunn" McMullin. Sinsel signed on as the band's singer, and they were joined by guitarist Guy Lacey and bassist Shawn Trotter. War Babies played gigs all over Seattle, opening for bands such as Mother Love Bone, Alice in Chains, and Soundgarden, looking for a record deal.

"When the Fifth Angel thing came about, it was something like, 'The band is signed to a major label and wants to do a video, so there maybe wasn't so much talk about joining forces right away,'" Stuverud said. "I was familiar with Ken Mary, but I didn't know any of the Fifth Angel guys, as it was a different scene."

Archer couldn't recall whether hiring Stuverud was strictly for the video, or if the band was hoping for a more permanent union. But the drummer was listed in Fifth Angel's fan club material at the time as the newest member of the band.

Pilot remembered Stuverud being a nice guy and good drummer, but the singer felt that Stuverud, and everyone who sought to play drums for the band, were doing so at a disadvantage. Pilot said the band expected everyone to play just like Ken Mary, and that wasn't a realistic approach. But Stuverud made the most of his time with Fifth Angel.

"My small experience with Fifth Angel was exciting," Stuverud said. "It was my first time in New York, and I think I even roomed with Ed when we shot the video. The song, 'Time Will Tell,' is killer. It's super cool. The album had a polished edge, but not super-polished, if you know what I mean. It was a new thing for me."

On the day of the video shoot, Stuverud planned to blend his punk rock roots and image with Fifth Angel's hard rock/heavy metal approach. Initially, he only wanted to use one kick drum for his kit. But he said Pilot asked him to use two. But he still flew the flag for punk music, rocking a CBGB T-shirt, paying homage to the legendary New York City club.

Macko could relate to Stuverud a bit, as the bassist was no stranger to playing a different genre of music. Macko had transitioned from pop to heavy metal just a few years prior. Macko recalled Stuverud being a good fit for Fifth Angel, at least initially.

"He was really good and played the songs pretty close to the way Ken played them," Macko said. "Unknown to us, however, Richard had slipped a demo tape of a band he was working with called War Babies to one of the Epic people, which I think was his main motivation for doing the video and joining Fifth Angel."

Stuverud recalls his experience with Fifth Angel positively. The video shoot was his first trip to New York City, and the chance to be in a video with the band helped open doors for him. But he was adamant that the situation with War Babies was proceeding at its own pace, on its own merits, and he wasn't using the opportunity with Fifth Angel to push his other band along.

"I think what was a challenge for me at that time, was oh shit, I have this opportunity with Fifth Angel and Epic Records, but War Babies was being looked at by Nick Terzo, who signed Alice in Chains," Stuverud said. "So, I don't necessarily think it was anything like me using my connections with Fifth Angel to see what I can do with War Babies. I think, from my memory, that the War Babies experience was evolving as well, and it was just interesting timing. I even remember Kendall Bechtel saying to me, 'Hey man, you gotta decide, bro. I don't think it's gonna work with you being in two bands.' It was a tough call."

Stuverud made the decision to leave Fifth Angel in 1990, and War Babies signed a deal with Columbia Records in 1991. War Babies released its self-titled album in 1992 and disbanded in 1993. A second album by the band, *Vault*, which is comprised of unreleased recordings from the 1990s, was issued by NW Metalworx Music in 2024.

As for Fifth Angel, *Time Will Tell* was out in stores, three years after Fifth Angel's debut. But promotion of the latest LP was limited. A second video was planned for "Broken Dreams," but it was never green lit by Epic Records. But with a new era of music blossoming at home in Seattle, some members of Fifth Angel found themselves at a career crossroads in 1990.

A magazine advertisement for *Time Will Tell*.

Ken Mary tracking drums for *Time Will Tell*.
Photos courtesy of Ed Archer.

Terry Brown, Ed Archer, Ted Pilot, John Macko, and Kendall Bechtel in early 1989.

Fifth Angel Manager Derek Simon in early 1989 at Mediasound in New York City.

Fifth Angel visiting the original World Trade Center in New York City.
Photos by and courtesy of Kendall Bechtel.

Kendall Bechtel at Carriage House Studios, in Stamford, Connecticut.
Photo courtesy of Ed Archer.

The front and back covers of Fifth Angel's *Time Will Tell*, autographed by John Macko, Kendall Bechtel, Ted Pilot, Ken Mary, and Ed Archer, to the author.

The only promotional photo of Fifth Angel to feature Richard Stuverud. From left to right: Stuverud, Kendall Bechtel, Ted Pilot, Ed Archer, and John Macko. Photo courtesy of Ted Pilot.

A collage of images from Fifth Angel's "Time Will Tell" video.

Fifth Angel as photographed by Marty Temme in New York, circa 1989.
Photos by and courtesy of Marty Temme.

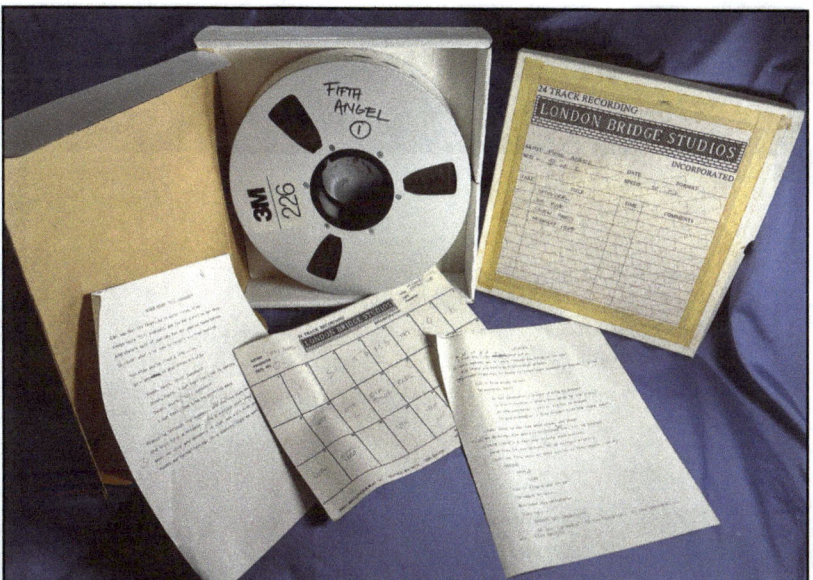

Fifth Angel's *Time Will Tell* demo recordings, which were tracked at London Bridge Studios, in Shoreline, Washington. Photo by and courtesy of Ed Archer.

The track sheet for recording the demo of "Midnight Love" from *Time Will Tell*. Image courtesy of Ed Archer.

CATHEDRAL

A A♭ F♯ A♭ F♯ *calling*

I fear the fire, ~~burning~~ down below.

A Dark desire, as it tears through the flesh of my soul.

And there's a feeling, hiding deep within.

It's Always fighting, to bleed my heart when temptation begins - Oh No

    You'll find a way to me-

    To reach my soul-

        In the cathedral - voices crying to heaven

        In the cathedral - where they pray to the light

        In the cathedral - voices crying to heaven

        In the cathedral - they escape from the night again.

I hear them lying, see them cheat and steal

THERE No denying, the endless bloodshed *that* they try to conceal

→ (And there's a feeling, hiding deep within)

  (And they're not driven, to be changed within)

  (But) be forgiven, so they can do it over again - oh no

    BRIDGE

        CHORUS

            LEAD

    You'll fing a way to me-

    To reach my soul.

    Now hear the whispers-

    They call - - -

        CHORUS OUT (Modulated)

        In the Cathedral, In the Cathedral, In the Cathedral....
etc. High part???

The lyric sheet used to record a demo of "Cathedral" from *Time Will Tell*.

The initial handwritten lyrics of "Midnight Love" from *Time Will Tell*. Image courtesy of Ed Archer.

The Taiwanese cassette version of Fifth Angel's *Time Will Tell*.

Video Shoot Itinerary

Fifth Angel's Itinerary From the 'Time Will Tell' Video Shoot

The following is Fifth Angel's travel itinerary from when the band traveled to New York to film the video for "Time Will Tell" in October 1989. The original is two pages long and printed on "Simon Says Incorporated" letterhead. The text has been reproduced as closely as possible to the original.

FIFTH ANGEL NEW YORK ITINERARY

Thursday, October 26th

Northwest Flt.#483 (from Detroit) arrives at LaGuardia Airport at 6:04pm.

Epic Records has arranged for a car to take the band to Southgate Towers Hotel, 371 Seventh Avenue (at 31st Street).

Hotel phone number – (212)563-1800.

Carol Radel will meet the band at the hotel.

9:45pm "Shocker" premier, theater between 2nd and 3rd Avenue on 59th Street. Movie starts at 10:15pm. Band may be listed on guest list as FIFTH ANGEL or under individual names. Carol Radel is on the guest list as well. If there are any problems, ask for Ann Stivola/Universal at the box office.

The band will also be on the guest list at The Cat Club (76 E. 13th St.) where Vain are playing.

Friday, October 27th

Ted and Kendall should be at Epic Records by 12:00pm. (51 W. 52nd Street, 13th Floor) for press.

Ed, John and Richard are free until 3:00pm, when they should also be at Epic Records to meet and take photos with the Epic Records staff.

There will be a dinner with the Epic Records staff around 6:00pm.

Carol Radel will be available with the band virtually all day.

The evening after dinner is free. Various shows around New York.

NOTE: Ed and Kendall should make time to go by ESP Guitars 9170 W. 48th Street, 3rd Fl. – very near Epic Records) to borrow guitars for the video shoot.

Saturday, October 28th

Free day to be used for last minute preparations for video. We may want to visit clothing stores in the

Village.

Ted may be needed for some preliminary shooting, but this is doubtful.

The band should also leave some free time in the early afternoon to drop by the CMJ convention at the Vista Hotel (3 World Trade Center – way downtown).

Dinner with Derek around 11:00pm. Various shows around New York after dinner.

Sunday, October 29th

10:00am talent call. You must be on set at the video location by this time. **All** gear and clothing that you need must come with you at this time. Main gear will be at location before you arrive.

Location: 172 Norfolk Street (just south of Houston, between Avenue A and Avenue B).

Be prepared to be on set until 12:00am. There are full facilities at the location.

Monday, October 30th

Hotel check out by 1:00pm. (Late check-out, will be pre-arranged.)

Car service will pick band up at hotel by 1:15pm to go to Newark airport.

The location where Fifth Angel shot the video for "Time Will Tell" as it appeared in 2022.

John Macko and Richard Stuverud on the set of Fifth Angel's "Time Will Tell" video. Photo courtesy of Fifth Angel.

Kendall Bechtel on the set of the "Time Will Tell" video.

> "Can't get beyond the wall that would set me free..."
>
> – Fifth Angel, "Broken Dreams"

Chapter 6
Into Waiting Darkness

The planned second single from *Time Will Tell*, "Broken Dreams," never did get the music video treatment, but the song was still featured by Epic Records in 1990. The track was a part of *A Wake-Up Call For The '90s Epic/Associated Hard Rock Sampler*, a compilation featuring artists such as Ozzy Osbourne, Alice Cooper, and some other heavy hitters like Prong, Sanctuary and Suicidal Tendencies. An edited version of "Broken Dreams" (cut down slightly for radio play) was the eighth track on the release.

But the writing was on the wall for Fifth Angel. Once again, the band needed a drummer, tour offers were non-existent, and much of the marketing promised to the group for *Time Will Tell* was not happening. In addition, CBS Records Group (which Epic Records was under) was sold to Sony Corporation in January 1988. After two years of restructuring, much of the A&R team at the band's label was now completely different. People who didn't work with Fifth Angel previously were now helping determine the band's future.

On top of that, even local heavy music fans in Seattle and critics were starting to shun the band, which frustrated Pilot at the time.

"Some people in the area feel like we haven't been through all the shit of playing clubs like the Riviera and stuff. But we did that scene for years," Pilot said, referring to Ridge, in an interview with Andrea Long and Michele Klossner. "Geoff Tate and I were in a battle of the bands together, years ago. We've been there too."

Fifth Angel tried one last time to tour, however. The band decided if they couldn't get on the road with a bigger act, that they would go out themselves and headline small clubs. The first date was supposed to be on January 16, 1990, in Portland, Oregon.

Archer recalled Simon working with a booking agency to secure dates for Fifth Angel. But a lot of time passed while an itinerary was being worked out, and while the sales of *Time Will Tell* were okay, Epic started wondering why the band wasn't on the road to support the record.

"I remember the tentative dates of the headline tour and there were a lot of nights we were not playing," Archer said. "Usually, you play three or four nights in a row, and then a day off. From what I recall, the tour was structured so we would play two nights, and then we'd be off two nights, or we would play three nights in a row, and then not have another gig until four days later. I remember thinking that we weren't going to play as much as we should be, in order for it to be self-sustaining. And then the label pulled back tour support, and that was the beginning of the end."

Fifth Angel was also questioning if they had the right management at the time. The band discussed signing with more formidable management companies, the logic being that the bigger the company, the more likely it was they could get Fifth Angel on a tour. But it just didn't work out.

Thinking back, Archer feels one of Fifth Angel's major missteps was not having a tour planned before the release of

Time Will Tell. Had they been on the road in fall 1989, Fifth Angel may have seen more marketing and financial support from the label. From Archer's perspective, a lot of things were done after the fact, which may have hampered the band's progress.

"Derek did a great job for us, he was really good at facilitating a lot of things for Fifth Angel," Archer said. "If it wasn't for him, we probably wouldn't have gotten a major label deal. But at the time, he was still learning and there were other management companies that we were told about. They knew of us, and they were interested. We didn't know what the right thing to do was. You don't want to hurt somebody's feelings who took us to where we were at, but if we wanted to get to the next level, we thought about going a different direction."

Ultimately, Fifth Angel stayed the course with Simon. After pulling tour support, Epic/CBS wanted Fifth Angel to start fresh with a third album. And while the band had some new material written, they were proud of *Time Will Tell* and wanted to see the record get a real chance to succeed. As a result, forced with the prospect of going right back into the studio, the allure of continuing as Fifth Angel was waning for a couple of the band members.

Archer did some soul searching and decided to leave the group. The guitarist explained he became very disillusioned with the industry in early 1990. When Epic pulled back tour support and marketing money from Fifth Angel, Archer saw the end was nigh.

"It was scary and depressing and I was thinking that there really are no guarantees with the music business, and it was a role of the dice," Archer said, reflecting on his thought process at the end of the *Time Will Tell* record cycle. "I was getting concerned about being able to support myself financially with music. We were kind of there, but from my perspective, I was getting older, and at this point I had already gone back to school and had my backup plan in place, working in electronics. That stemmed from my interest in how the guitar works, and wanting to know how sound is created and altered by the strings and pickups. Ironically, Randy Hemming, who helped us with the demo recordings for the first Fifth Angel album, was my boss. Anyway, for me, with things stalling out with music, I wasn't sure what the future had in store for the band, because it wasn't feeling right. It was like we missed the boat with things. We took it to a great level and felt we all should be proud of what we achieved, but I wasn't sure a breakthrough was going to happen."

Archer recalled a recent conversation he had with Ken Mary, where the two discussed the choices made by the band in 1990. According to Archer, the drummer told him that in some ways, the members of Fifth Angel were "too smart for their own good" back then, not taking the risks that may have led them to stardom.

"It seems to me in hindsight, that oftentimes the bands who take the risks and are in the moment—then it happens," Archer said. "But for all those success stories, there are a lot of stories where it didn't work out and people are destitute and older and still trying to make it. I've known some of those people, and now they are in their 50s and 60s, and it's a sad story. That's not the life I wanted, nor Ted."

Losing Archer was a significant blow to Fifth Angel. The guitarist was one of the primary songwriters in the group. But the band, at least initially, had every intention of carrying on. Stuverud had also left to pursue War Babies, but Fifth Angel had a line on a great drummer, courtesy of a recommendation from Ken Mary—John Luke Hébert.[20] Hébert had just finished recording *Shock Waves*, the 1989 album by Leather.

"He's a really good drummer and came out to Seattle and we were rehearsing with him, and then it fell apart," Macko said, regarding Hébert. "Whoever was doing our booking couldn't put anything together."

"I was kind of freelancing at the time, and Ken said Fifth Angel was looking for a drummer," Hébert said. "They flew me out there, Kendall and Ted picked me up at the airport, and I think I stayed the first two nights with Kendall, and then two nights at Ted's dad's house. I got up there, and the second day we did the rehearsal—me, John, and Kendall, with Ted there—and everything was cool. Then a couple of days went by, and they got dropped by Epic, while I was there. That's exactly what happened. I was living in Dallas, but I was ready to start commuting back and forth and all of a sudden, I remember Ted saying, 'We just got dropped by Epic.' I was like, 'What does that mean?' He was like, 'Probably the end of things.' I remember that vividly."

Ted Pilot's exit from Fifth Angel was not far behind. The singer was pursuing his college education at Seattle University the entire time he was in the band. Pilot recalled doing physics homework at Steve Lawson Productions between vocal takes when the band was recording *Fifth Angel*. Ted graduated magna cum laude in 1987. He then applied to the University of Washington School of Dentistry and got in.

But after Fifth Angel signed with Epic, part of the contract

---

20. Jeffrey McCormack, a drummer who would play an important role with Fifth Angel many years later, auditioned for the band in 1990. McCormack said his skill level wasn't where it needed to be back then, and he didn't get the gig.

specifically stated that none of the band members could be a student or have a full-time job. In a nutshell, the record contract made Pilot devote himself entirely to the band. Back then, such a clause in a record contract was seen as reasonable, given the amount of money labels invested in making records.

"I was at a precipice where I had already taken two years off of school," Pilot said. "I had already taken the National Board Dental Examination. If I had taken one more year off, I would have to start all over again in dental school."

Pilot was conflicted about what to do, but he finally chose his dental career over music and stepped away from Fifth Angel in 1990.

"The decision had nothing to do with the band at all, they were awesome," Pilot added. "It's not that I wanted to stop singing. I just had to take a break from it."

Losing Pilot created a void that Simon felt was the death knell for Fifth Angel.

"Without Ted, the band would not have been as special," Simon said. "Melodically, I loved what they did, the twin guitar stuff with James and Ed, and Kendall, who is an amazing player and a great human being. But I don't know if the band would have been as exceptional to me without Ted Pilot."

The group looked for new members for a short while after that. Replacing Archer and Pilot was ultimately not fruitful, and Fifth Angel disbanded.

Macko was irate at the time. He recalled being angry at his bandmates for giving up on their musical aspirations after having put so much work into the Fifth Angel.

"I was pissed because I was a full-time musician at that point," Macko said. "Look, every musician, their dream is to get signed and become a big rock star. I thought when we signed that contract with Epic, that it was all downhill from there. I thought, 'Okay, this is it. I'm going to be in the big time.' I just watched my dream go up in smoke. I was really disgruntled about that. I still am to this day, but you have to let things go."

As fate would have it, Fifth Angel's profile may have exploded later in 1990, had they still been together. Radio personality Howard Stern had been making quite a stir as the host of a morning show on WXRK in New York City for almost four years. The show was also simulcast on stations in Philadelphia and Washington D.C. But Stern was looking at television opportunities, and he found one with WWOR-TV, based in Secaucus, New Jersey.

Stern and WWOR-TV reached a deal for a TV program, *The Howard Stern Show*. Hosted by Stern and Robin Quivers, the show debuted on July 14, 1990, and expanded later that year. It received national syndication in January 1991 and lasted until August 1992 before ending. Fifth Angel's "Midnight Love" was used as the intro music to the program throughout its entire run.

Unfortunately, Fifth Angel was no longer together, and couldn't capitalize on the exposure that *The Howard Stern Show* provided the band. Royalty payments for use of "Midnight Love" eventually started coming in, which is when the band members found out about it.

"I remember watching Howard Stern's show and I thought 'Midnight Love' as his intro was pretty cool," Pilot said.

Simon was obviously disappointed when Fifth Angel got dropped by Epic Records. In retrospect, however, he wished both he and the band would have made some different decisions along the way, which may have altered the trajectory for Fifth Angel in the 1990s.

"Getting a major label deal, the feeling is like, 'We've made it, it's going to happen,' Simon said, reflecting on Fifth Angel's journey. "The music is so good, we're on a major, it's not RCA, not a secondary, it's fucking CBS Records, Epic Records. But if they're not actively working to make it happen with you, and for you, it just wasn't gonna happen. I have very fond memories of the time, but we could have done so much more to help ourselves. Whether that was forcing people to make decisions to leave jobs or this or that, and who knows if they ever would have. There was no doubt Ted was going to dental school, and Ed had his gig. But, if you ask me what comes to mind when I hear the name Fifth Angel, it's 'What could have been.'"

The members of Fifth Angel went their separate ways in 1990, and life took a very different turn for some of them. Ken Mary, however, is the only one who has been a full-time musician. Once his initial tenure with Fifth Angel was over in 1989, he went on to a very successful career as a session drummer, recording six albums with Impellitteri, three records with House of Lords, and several collaborations with other bands and recording artists.

One of Ken's crowning achievements in the years that followed his departure from Fifth Angel was the establishment of his own recording studio. SonicPhish Productions, located in Mesa, Arizona, is a state-of-the-art facility, whose clients include artists from Warner Bros. Entertainment, ABC, MCA Records, CBS Broadcasting, Rhino Records, and many others.

Ken is still active as a drummer. He is currently a full-time member of the heavy metal band Flotsam and Jetsam, which will be discussed further in the pages ahead.

James Byrd began an incredible creative run as a solo artist after his time in Fifth Angel was over. From 1990-2002, Byrd released seven studio albums. Full of neo-classical guitar solos and emotive vocals by various singers, Byrd's records are auditory adventures. The first four releases from Byrd were on Shrapnel Records and Roadrunner.

Ken Mary played drums on Byrd's first offering, *James Byrd's Atlantis Rising*, which was released by Shrapnel. According to Byrd, a few of the tracks that appear on the album were initially slated for Fifth Angel's second effort, *Time Will Tell*. Those songs are: "Fly to The Sun," "Fallen Warrior," "Angel of Mercy," and "Into the Light." Ironically, *Time Will Tell* contains a track called "Angel of Mercy," but the two songs are completely different in all but the title.

There is one instance where the music on *Fifth Angel* and *James Byrd's Atlantis Rising*[21] overlaps, however. Listen closely to the intro of Fifth Angel's "Cry Out the Fools" and then put "Fly to The Sun" on at the 14-second mark. Sound familiar? The similarity is likely just a coincidence, but it certainly illustrates how vital and distinct Byrd's playing was on the first Fifth Angel album.

The connections to Fifth Angel continued a decade later.

---

21. *James Byrd's Atlantis Rising* features Freddy Krumins on vocals. But according to Tim Branom, Krumins and Byrd had some issues at the time, so Byrd had Branom lined up to sing on the project if Krumins didn't pan out. "They brought me in, and I had to hire an attorney and sign a letter of intent saying I'd sign the contract [to sing] if they needed me," Branom said. "That was pretty weird. It was all sneaky."

Byrd's 1998 record, *Crimes of Virtuosity*, featured a singer named Kendall Torrey. The vocalist was actually guitarist Kendall Bechtel, who replaced Byrd in Fifth Angel. Bechtel used his middle name as his surname in the album liner notes to avoid an obvious connection to his old band.

Byrd also started a guitar company, designing and building the Byrd Super Avianti, which features a Balance Compensated Wing body. Byrd was completely hands-on in developing the prototypes. The guitar has a few innovative features, including an option to give players a uniquely scalloped finger board, called "Use Delineated Compound" (U.D.C.) scalloping.

The guitarist has been largely absent from music since 2002, although Lion Music put out a compilation of his work, *Beyond the Pillars*, in 2011.

John Macko said he was in a bit of a "fog" for the first couple of years following Fifth Angel's breakup. The bassist was still playing in a cover band that was gigging around Seattle, albeit on a part-time basis. But the music scene in the Emerald City was changing in the early 1990s, morphing to a genre the media labeled "grunge."

One of the first things Macko did after Fifth Angel was writing music with guitarist Jeff Loomis. Loomis was a family friend. Macko recalled he and his then-wife babysitting the future guitar hero when Loomis was just a kid. Loomis would go on to play with Sanctuary briefly, and then make a name for himself in Nevermore, and later, as a solo artist and guitarist in Arch Enemy.

But the project between Macko and Loomis didn't pan out.

"I tried to put a band together with material that I was

CH6 | INTO WAITING DARKNESS

writing with Jeff Loomis and Gary Thompson from Q5," Macko said in 2007. "I was writing this heavy progressive stuff that at the time [that] no one was interested in. We did some demos but couldn't find a singer ... and after about a year of failed projects, I got burned out on the whole thing."

Macko knew his music career was at a crossroads, and he had more pressing concerns. His daughter, Madison, was born in July 1990. John ended up as a stay-at-home dad for a bit, before his stepdad convinced him to go back to school.

At first, Macko was intimidated. He'd been playing in bands since he was in high school, and other than construction, the musician didn't have any job skills. John enrolled in a community college in Seattle, completing a few semesters of work toward an accounting degree. But he eventually switched to the school's computer program, and that's when John found his professional calling.

Macko spent almost 30 years working in the information technology field. The bassist admitted that his evolution from a musician to a white-collar professional was not easy, but it was clearly the right choice for him.

"I'm really grateful my path went that way," Macko said. "Even though some of my hopes and dreams were crushed, looking at where I'm at now, I'm 66 years old and I can play music if I want to, not because I have to. There's no pressure."

Macko eventually relocated to Florida, where he's lived ever since.

Kendall Bechtel continued with his music career after Fifth Angel disbanded. One of his first projects was Sweet Sister

Sam, featuring singer Steve Benito. Benito joined Heir Apparent in 1987 and made a name for himself as the vocalist on the band's second album, *One Small Voice*. But by 1990, Benito's run with Heir Apparent was over, and he and Bechtel connected.

Bechtel, Benito, keyboardist Randy Gane (who played in the local band Myth, and was also Queensrÿche's touring keyboardist in 1986-1987), bassist Michael Crouse, and drummer Michael Tapogna got together and started writing songs. They recorded a demo at Robert Lang Studios in Shoreline, Washington, featuring songs such as "Time Heals All" and "After the Fall." Gane gave the tape to Queensrÿche guitarist Michael Wilton, who liked it and passed it along to EMI Records (Queensrÿche's label at the time). Sweet Sister Sam was invited to open for Queensrÿche for a few shows in late 1991 in the Pacific Northwest.

Although Sweet Sister Sam worked diligently, recording more songs, and playing the Seattle club scene in the early 1990s, the band never landed a record deal. Sweet Sister Sam called it quits sometime in late 1994. Bechtel continued playing in a variety of bands and projects over the years, including singing on the previously mentioned *Crimes of Virtuosity* by James Byrd.

Ted Pilot finished dental school in 1993, earning a doctorate in dental surgery and graduating with honors. He attained a certificate in endodontics in 1995, and opened his own practice, Pacific Endodontics, in August 1995. Ted practiced for almost 22 years before moving on to other business interests. Pilot is currently the chief executive officer of a manufacturing company based in Kent, Washington.

Ed Archer spent time after Fifth Angel using his hands—and not on a guitar. The guitarist packed away his instruments and set to work designing and building his home in a suburb of Seattle. Archer still lives there today with his family. Career-wise, Archer earned a degree in electronics and as mentioned previously, he went to work in that field. He's still working in that industry in 2025.

A hype sticker for Fifth Angel's *Time Will Tell*.

A WAKE-UP CALL FOR THE '90s: Epic/Associated Hard Rock Sampler

1. Ozzy Osbourne "WAR PIGS"*** (8:23)
2. Alice Cooper "TRASH" (4:02)
3. Killer Dwarfs "DIRTY WEAPONS"* (3:38)
4. Shark Island "PARIS CALLING" (4:50)
5. Suicidal Tendencies "WAKING THE DEAD" (6:53)
6. Prong "DYING BREED"* (3:26)
7. Sanctuary "FUTURE TENSE"* (5:07)
8. Fifth Angel "BROKEN DREAMS" (Edit) (4:14)
9. Danger Danger "BANG BANG" (3:56)
10. Gothic Slam "WHO DIED AND MADE YOU GOD" (4:30)
11. Meliah Rage "KILL TO SURVIVE" (2:44)
12. Kreator "SOME PAIN WILL LAST" (5:38)
13. Johnny Crash "HEY KID"* (3:27)
14. Riot "KILLER"* (4:52)
15. Beau Nasty "LOVE TO THE BONE" (4:51)

A Wake-Up Call For The '90s featured a radio edit version of Fifth Angel's "Broken Dreams."

An autographed promotional photo of James Byrd from the late-1980s/early-1990s.

In His Words

Ed Archer on Fifth Angel's First Trip to New York City

Back in the 1980s, Seattle was a "sleepy little town" that nobody seemed to care much about or had even heard of. This was before the internet and before Amazon. Companies like Starbucks and Microsoft were still fairly new and pretty small back then.

But there we were, having hit the "big time" with Fifth Angel's recording contract with Epic Records, arriving in New York City in early 1989 after doing pre-production in Seattle for *Time Will Tell* with Rush producer Terry Brown. In reality, we were just a bunch of punks from the Pacific Northwest, traveling to the Big Apple for the very first time. Talk about culture shock!

Ted was in charge of the "band money," and he brought a good amount of it to New York, in cash. He was apparently very intrigued by the sidewalk game where the dude hides a pea in a walnut shell and shuffles around two other shells while onlookers try to guess which of the three shells has the pea in it! Ted, bless him, didn't realize that it was a scam! There were plants in the crowd who were part of the hustle, with them correctly guessing where the pea was to lure in unsuspecting folks to place bets and try to find the pea. The plants made it look easy, but when someone took the bait and placed a bet, that's when the *real* game started! Using quick sleight-of-hand or whatever else they did, they made it impossible to find where the pea was! Ha!

Suffice it to say, poor Ted lost a lot of our band money to that hustle! I didn't hear about this until after-the-fact, but Ted was freaking out, so he found a bank to withdraw his personal money and reimbursed the band's money that he'd lost! We were just oblivious to how things worked on the streets of Manhattan. Live and learn!

Ted Pilot and Kendall Bechtel signing Fifth Angel promo photos in New York City. Photo courtesy of Kendall Bechtel.

> "We watch you. We see you.
> We'll tell you what is real.
> No running, nowhere to hide."
>
> — Fifth Angel, "We Rule"

Chapter 7
Resurrection

Rumors of a possible Fifth Angel reunion surfaced in late-2006/early-2007. *FifthAngel.net*, which was then a website founded by this author to archive the band's history, was noticed by the group's alumni. This led to some initial contact and discussions about Fifth Angel's dissolution in 1990.

When Bechtel was asked about Fifth Angel reforming, the guitarist said at the time that a reunion "would be a blast," and that he "would be only too happy to deliver." Macko shared similar sentiments to Bechtel, but doubted Pilot would be a part of things.

As it turned out, Archer and Pilot had already talked about the possibility of playing some shows. But neither of them had done anything in music since leaving Fifth Angel in 1990, and family and professional commitments didn't allow either of them the flexibility to seriously entertain the idea.

"I discussed touring with Ed at length, and he felt that touring, especially the preparation, would result in too much time being taken away from his son," Pilot said in 2007. "He's a good father and has a nice family. I think that's a justifiably good reason not to tour.

"It's maybe not as noble [a reason as Ed], but I am busy running my practice," Pilot added. "If everything is not lined up, the additional time I would be required to spend would not be doable."

While the real and speculative chatter about Fifth Angel did not result in anything tangible then, it did whet the appetite of fans who were interested in seeing the band perform. Just a few years later, an unexpected call led to Fifth Angel finally getting back together.

In 2009, Oliver Weinsheimer, the organizer and promoter of Keep it True, an annual German heavy metal festival, reached out to John Macko. Having been a Fifth Angel fan since 1988, Weinsheimer wanted to gauge the group's interest in reuniting and performing at Keep it True. Weinsheimer offered Fifth Angel a headline slot at the festival. Macko was floored by the proposal. He was shocked that anyone would still be interested in the band after it was dormant for almost 20 years.

Weinsheimer assured Macko that Fifth Angel had an audience in Germany who was eager to hear the band play. Once convinced, John called all his old bandmates from the *Time Will Tell* era. In the two years since the original reunion rumors surfaced, the schedules and lives of Pilot and Archer had calmed to a point where they could seriously entertain playing music again. As a result, everyone was willing to see if they could put Fifth Angel back together for the show, except for drummer Ken Mary.

That may seem odd, considering out of all the members of Fifth Angel, Mary was the one who made a full-time career in the music industry. But that was exactly why he passed on the opportunity to play with Fifth Angel in 2009.

"I was running a very successful recording studio at that point," Mary said, referring to SonicPhish Productions. "That was our heyday, and I was working and had an assistant. I would produce music from 9 a.m. to 6 p.m., trying to keep banker's hours. Then my assistant took over from 6 p.m. to 2 a.m. We were working sometimes seven days a week."

With Archer, Bechtel, Macko and Pilot on board, they started to discuss writing new music, in addition to playing live. The musicians were elated that people were still interested in Fifth Angel and issued a news release on March 24, 2009, stating their intention to be a "part-time" band that would write new music and play sporadic shows as schedules permitted.

"[J]ust know that the entire band appreciates every fan out there that has said such complimentary things about our music over the past 20 years," Fifth Angel said in the statement. "We've seen the comments on Amazon.com and YouTube, read the e-mails and observed all the discussion on message boards on the internet. We know bands say this all the time, but we truly are humbled by your enthusiasm for our music, particularly after being disbanded for so long. It means a lot to us."

Before they could get started in earnest, however, Fifth Angel needed to settle on a drummer for the new era of the band. The one they selected was right in their backyard and happened to be very familiar with their music—Jeffrey McCormack.

Jeffrey McCormack was born in the late 1960s. His family moved to Seattle in 1978, and music was deeply embedded in their DNA. McCormack's uncle was a pianist who taught at the Cornish College of the Arts in Seattle. He gave Jeffrey his first piano lesson at age nine. Young Jeffrey loved playing music but disliked taking lessons. But instead of his uncle getting angry, he gave Jeffrey two things that sparked his love of music—a chance to play drums, and tickets to a KISS concert.

November 21, 1979, at Seattle Center Coliseum changed McCormack's life forever. KISS was in town to support their latest album, *Dynasty*, and Jeff was in awe at what he saw.

"Seeing Peter Criss with this huge drum kit up on the riser and blowing stuff up ... was pretty much it for me, and I told my uncle I wanted to do that," McCormack said.

Jeff started learning how to play drums and signed up for all the music classes he could at school. Eventually, a student of Jeff's uncle, who was a drummer taking piano lessons, offered to teach Jeff. That's when McCormack's percussion skills started to surface.

John Bonham, Bobby Rondinelli, Cozy Powell, and Ian Paice were the early influences on McCormack's playing style. They were followed later in the 1980s by guys like Tommy Lee, Mick Brown and Tommy Aldridge, who all left a permanent impression on McCormack.

In the early 1980s, Jeff formed a series of garage bands, including Rival, which played at high schools and various talent shows. But in August 1984, he was in a band called Juvenile, which rehearsed at The Fun Hole, located in the Fremont area of Seattle. As McCormack walked into the facility to start rehearsal, another band was practicing (only one band could use the room at a time). That group was TKO, and with them was drummer Ken Mary.

McCormack described watching Mary play as "mesmerizing" and he became a massive fan of the drummer, and later, Mary's work with Fifth Angel.

"Watching Ken Mary play from really just a few feet away was an education worth millions of dollars," McCormack said. "He's a brilliant musician with passion, dynamics, unbelievable technique and extraordinary showmanship. I wanted to be that kind of drummer."

McCormack continued honing his skills in the mid-1980s. Juvenile eventually found singer Tim Branom and the band played its first show in March 1985. The group moved rehearsals to the "Hell House," located at 4419 Fremont North, in Seattle. They shared the band house with Serpent's Knight, a band that featured vocalist Warrel Dane, who would go on to fame with both Sanctuary and Nevermore a few years later.

Juvenile played dates throughout 1985 and eventually morphed into a band called Sentence, which lasted until Branom departed to form Gypsy Rose in late-1986/early-1987. McCormack gigged around a bit and worked at The Music Bank, the famous warehouse with 60 rehearsal rooms that were used as living and practice spaces for several iconic Seattle bands. McCormack occasionally jammed with Jerry Cantrell and Layne Staley who would go on to form Alice in Chains.

Eventually, McCormack hooked up with Rick Pierce, the guitarist of Q5, and joined his new band, Nightshade. McCormack played drums on the group's debut, *Dead of Night*, which was released in 1991. McCormack eventually stepped down from Nightshade for various personal reasons, including providing care for his terminally ill brother.

In 2006, McCormack signed on with Heir Apparent for its European tour celebrating the 20th anniversary of the band's debut album, *Graceful Inheritance*. Heir Apparent played a warm-up show for that tour on October 28, 2006, at Lakepoint Bar & Grill in Kenmore, Washington. In attendance was Kendall Bechtel from Fifth Angel. McCormack and the guitarist got caught up, and Bechtel invited Jeff to come jam with him and Ed Archer when he returned from Heir Apparent's tour.

One of the shows on that tour was the Keep it True festival in Germany. McCormack had such a good time, he asked promoter Oliver Weinsheimer if there was anything he could do to connect him with bands from the Seattle area. One of the groups that Oliver wanted to talk to was Fifth Angel.

When McCormack returned to Seattle, he emailed the members of Fifth Angel, copying Weinsheimer on the discussions, trying to entice the band to reunite. In addition, McCormack cold-called Archer at his office (which surprised Archer's assistant, who had no idea about Ed's musical past), pitching him on the opportunity to get Fifth Angel back together and play some gigs. But as discussed previously, Archer passed, given his work and family commitments at the time, as did Pilot.

One thing McCormack wanted to make clear, however, was that while he was on tour with Heir Apparent, his complete focus was on performing that band's set to the best of his ability. Some rumors spread that Jeffrey only used the tour with Heir Apparent to reunite Fifth Angel, which the drummer steadfastly denies to this day.

McCormack wasn't the only drummer considered for the new era of Fifth Angel, however. Archer and Macko flew to Texas in February 2010 to audition John Luke Hébert, who, as mentioned earlier, rehearsed with Fifth Angel before the group broke up in 1990. The trio jammed at a studio in the Dallas area where Hébert had previously recorded some drums with King Diamond. But when the three musicians began to play, Archer said Hébert just wasn't up to speed on

Fifth Angel's songs, and it became obvious that McCormack was the right choice for the band.

When asked about that rehearsal, Hébert said he was very ill in the days before Archer and Macko flew into Dallas to jam, which affected his ability to get familiar with Fifth Angel's material and practice up.

"It was wintertime, and we had planned this trip for like a month," Hébert said. "But three days prior to that happening, I had low blood sugar and passed out cold. They hospitalized me for like six hours. So, the next couple of days I was weak and lethargic, but I couldn't cancel—they were coming. We played through the songs, and I really felt like a wreck. I just remember not feeling well and not playing my best. I told them that too. It was cold with snow on the ground in Dallas, it was just miserable timing."

In the end, McCormack got the drummer gig. But prior to figuring out their drummer situation, Archer, Bechtel, Macko, and Pilot needed to start rehearsing and refamiliarizing themselves with the nuances of Fifth Angel's music. With Macko in Florida, the bassist had to get ready on his own. But Archer, Bechtel, and Pilot were conveniently together in the Seattle area. Everyone was responding to emails regarding rehearsal schedules, except for Pilot. After some prompting and voice mails left by various members of Fifth Angel, the singer finally got in touch. Macko said Pilot told them all that given his increasingly busy schedule, he would not be able to go forward with the performance.

The members of Fifth Angel were crushed. But there was more to the story and the singer's reasoning than Pilot initially let on about.[22] But the band had no time to wait—they needed

---

22. Pilot's reason for not performing with Fifth Angel is discussed more thoroughly in the Epilogue.

to make sure they had a great replacement vocalist in time for its performance at Keep it True on April 24, 2010. Luckily, Archer had one in mind. The guitarist had been demoing new song ideas with an old friend: singer Tim Branom. Branom was living in Los Angeles, but with his roots in the Seattle metal and grunge scenes, it seemed like a natural fit.

Tim Branom was born on June 4, 1965, in Seattle. As mentioned earlier, the singer fronted the local Seattle metal bands Juvenile and Sentence, along with Gypsy Rose in the mid-1980s. Branom was a big fan of Ted Pilot, having followed Ridge as a teenager. Later, Branom would work for Pilot, as the latter singer gave vocal lessons once Fifth Angel got signed to a record deal. In addition, Pilot and Queensrÿche vocalist Geoff Tate were involved in a small business called "Vocalstar," where the singers provided vocal lessons on cassette, and people would purchase the series and have it mailed to them.

"I learned from Ted, and he did influence me a lot as a singer," Branom said. "Back in the early 80s, people said we sounded alike, except he was a few years older and well trained, and I was just a kid."[23]

Branom eventually relocated to Los Angeles in order to

---

23. Tim Branom wrote and recorded a song called "The Walk of the Dead" in 1984. The track featured singer Ted Pilot. Branom plays guitar and bass and programmed the drums. Ron Stokes played keyboards on the song, which was mixed at Steve Lawson Productions in December 1984. The song was never officially released, but it was performed by various bands that Branom was in during the 1980s (with Branom on vocals).

pursue his musical dreams. But by 1993, aspirations of having a "metal" band in Los Angeles seemed slim. Branom embraced a more classic rock vibe in a band called Cloud Nine, where he would sing, play guitar, bass, and keyboards. Cloud Nine continued for years, and Branom kept pushing his musical boundaries, working with a variety of artists. Tim also had a solo band, Branom, which picked up some significant interest in Japan.

Branom stayed active in several musical projects through 2010, notably working with future *American Idol* finalist Carly Smithson, who would later front the heavy rock band We Are the Fallen. But working with Ed Archer on new song ideas led Branom back to Fifth Angel. Branom was announced as Fifth Angel's new singer on January 12, 2010.[24]

"Recreating Ted Pilot's vocals in Fifth Angel brings me back to my roots of metal in the Seattle 1980s music scene where I grew up," Branom said in a press release. "I've known most of the members of Fifth Angel before they all played together."

Archer thought Branom had all the right talent and pedigree to follow in Pilot's footsteps, especially since both singers trained with the late Maestro David Kyle.

"When singing our music, his voice sounds eerily like Ted Pilot's did 20 years ago," Archer said, referring to Branom. "Throw in Tim's experience in the music business and he's exactly what we need moving forward to establish Fifth Angel as a force in heavy metal again. We couldn't be happier."

Archer picked up his guitar again in 2007-2008, mostly

---

24. This author was working with Fifth Angel in a media relations/spokesperson capacity during this time, drafting press releases and assisting the band with various issues.

to relieve stress from a busy professional life and a failing marriage at home. He called the initial songs he wrote "therapy" from everything he had going on at the time.

"Music became a diversion that got my brain, my synapses firing in a different kind of way, as a distraction to the shit I was dealing with, and it just kind of continued on," Archer said.

The rough demo songs Archer worked up for Fifth Angel included "Holocaust," "Wicca," "End of Days," "Last Rites," "Lost in Time," "No Way Out," "Soldier of Fortune – Wanderin' Gypsy," "Suicidal Tendency," and "The Unfaithful." These tunes were Archer's first foray back into songwriting since 1990. Branom recorded vocals on three other new tracks, "Voodoo Solution," "Sanctuary," and "Liar," so Archer could hear how he would sound over new material. Branom's voice worked, and it looked as if Fifth Angel had found their singer.

"These songs have much more ear candy, taboo subjects, and cool guitar riffs but all with the flair of previous Fifth Angel albums," Branom said at the time.

With Branom now in the fold, Fifth Angel made plans to get together at Archer's home in April 2010 for their official full band rehearsals in preparation for Keep it True. But several hurdles popped up that almost torpedoed Fifth Angel before the band's reunion got off the ground.

◀ GEOFF TATE
(of QUEENSRŸCHE)
AND
TED PILOT'S ▶
(of FIFTH ANGEL)

"VOCALSTAR"
ROCK/METAL VOCAL LESSONS

Over the past four years, these classic techniques have proven successful in helping **thousands** of vocalists take their voice *to the limit!!* Even if you're a guitarist, bassist, keyboardist or drummer, this series is for **YOU!** All bands want great background vocals, so **blow doors** at your next audition, improve your band's sound, or become the KICK ASS vocalist you've always dreamed of with **VOCALSTAR!!**

This professional step-by-step course is taught on cassette and fully explained in accompanying booklets. Each cassette is **packed** with information on different singing exercises and techniques that will **develop your power** like TED PILOT of FIFTH ANGEL, and enable you to **hit those sizzling high screams** like GEOFF TATE of QUEENSRŸCHE!!

THESE LESSONS ARE ALL YOU NEED TO TAKE YOUR VOICE OUT OF THE PRACTICE ROOM AND ONTO ARENA STAGES!!

Also, the **VOCALSTAR** course offers *vocal tips* on how to deal with problems encountered during singing. We're so sure that you'll benefit from this course that we offer a *full money back guarantee* on return of the lessons!! You *can't lose* with **VOCALSTAR!!**

Call (206) 746-8105 for more course information.

"This is the best vocal course I have ever encountered!! I used many of the same techniques found in the Vocalstar series to develop my own voice, and I strongly recommend this course for all singers!!" – Geoff Tate, Queensrÿche

"I took eight months of instruction in a similar method prior to sending for your course, but there were still things I didn't understand. Your course has shown me what I wanted to know!! Even the first few tapes made a noticeable difference in my delivery, not to mention my endurance. I can't believe how fast I am improving, and neither can my band! Thanks for a worthwhile product! My old teacher charged $20.00 per hour, and for the cost of three lessons you gave me everything I need to know to be a major talent. Thank you very, very much!"
Vince Byars, Colusa, CA

"Being a singer, I felt that I had been exposed to any and all techniques known to man. Boy, was I wrong!! In the short time I have had the course, my deliverance has improved, my endurance has increased, and my range has increased a half-octave!! I think the 'VOCALSTAR' series is EXCELLENT, and I recommend it to anyone who is looking to safely improve their voice!!" Kelly Miller, WGTA Radio, Summerville, GA

PACKAGE A: RECEIVE LESSONS 1, 2 AND 3 WHICH CONTAIN THE ESSENTIAL FOUNDATION FOR ALL SINGING! $29.00
LESSON ONE: Breath Control - The correct techniques for the control of breath and achieving powerful diaphragm support! LESSON TWO: Pronunciation - Techniques and exercises to teach correct pronunciation of vowels and consonants! And LESSON THREE: Tonal Placement - Demonstrating correct placement of the voice and how to achieve full resonance!

PACKAGE B: RECEIVE LESSONS 4, 5, 6 AND 7 WHICH CONTAIN A COMPLETE VOCAL EXERCISE PROGRAM ALONG WITH SCREAM TECHNIQUE!! $39.00
LESSON FOUR: Exercises Level I - Introductory vocal exercises and scales, practice guide. LESSON FIVE: Exercises Level II - Intermediate vocal exercises and scales (Part I), practice guide including scales from lesson four. LESSON SIX: Exercises Level III - Intermediate vocal exercises and scales (Part II), practice guide including scales from lessons four and five. And LESSON SEVEN: Exercises Level IV - SCREAM TECHNIQUE and advanced vocal exercises and scales, practice guide including all previous scales!

PACKAGE C: ENTIRE COURSE SPECIAL! THIS OFFER INCLUDES ALL LESSONS AND BOOKLETS ORGANIZED IN A PROTECTIVE BLACK TAPE BINDER. ALONG WITH A SPECIAL EIGHTH LESSON!! YOU WILL RECEIVE THE ENTIRE COURSE IN ONE PACKAGE TO LEARN AT YOUR OWN PACE!! $69.00
LESSON EIGHT: Vocal Techniques - How to prepare and what to expect in the studio and in live situations. Demonstrations of different studio effects on the voice and much more!! An essential lesson for the aspiring professional!!

Send To:
PM PRODUCTIONS
P.O. Box 40298
Bellevue, WA 98004
USA

Name
Street   Apt.
City
State   Zip
Country

Foreign countries, (except Canada) add $2.00 per lesson. All payments incl. Canada must be in U.S. funds. Please add $1.00 for shipping and handling. Order as many lessons as you like and still add only $1. Make checks payable to PM Productions. Allow three weeks for checks to clear. MONEY ORDERS ARE PROCESSED IMMEDIATELY!

$1

TOTAL

Copyright 1989 PM Productions

DON'T PUT OFF YOUR SUCCESS ANY LONGER - <u>ACT TODAY!!</u>

"Vocalstar" advertisement and cassette lesson.
Images courtesy of Brian L. Naron.

Tim Branom on January 7, 2010. Photo by Jeff Ellingson. Photo courtesy of Tim Branom.

Unused test photos of Ed Archer, John Macko, Jeffrey McCormack, and Kendall Bechtel of Fifth Angel. These were taken on March 6, 2010. Photos courtesy of Tim Branom.

Ed Archer working on new Fifth Angel songs and sound effects, circa 2009-2010.
Photos courtesy of Ed Archer.

New Fifth Angel T-shirt designs, circa 2010.
Images courtesy of Tim Branom.

> "Cold is the night, as the time grows near. As we wait, as we hide, from the fallout."
>
> - Fifth Angel, "In the Fallout"

Chapter 8
Day Into Night

Macko and Branom flew to Seattle in April 2010 to rehearse with Fifth Angel and visit old friends in the area. The band was enthusiastic about the upcoming show in Germany and looking forward to what the future might hold for them.

Rehearsals took place in Archer's basement. Fifth Angel initially came up with a 16-song setlist for their first-ever public live performance, consisting of eight tracks from both *Fifth Angel* and *Time Will Tell*. That was modified slightly, almost from the outset, with the band choosing to eliminate "Angel of Mercy" to make sure they did not go over their time limit, given the normal pauses bands take between songs to tune, and general stage banter.

According to Macko, the first day of rehearsal started out promising, with the band running through "The Night" and "In the Fallout." But by track three, "Shout it Out," Branom was having issues with his voice.

"He got through two songs and on the third song, he can't hit some of the notes and was pulling really far away from the microphone," Macko said. "I looked at Ed and Ed's eyes—I could just see that look, like, 'Oh, my God.'"

By the fourth song, "Cathedral," Archer pulled the plug

on Branom singing for the day. Macko said Branom told the band that he had been up early in the morning, which could have impacted his voice. Archer told Branom to rest, while the band played through the rest of the set instrumentally. They made plans for Tim to sing the following day.

Macko, who, like Branom, was staying with Archer, recalled hearing Branom later in the day running through vocal scales. Archer was alarmed that Tim was trying to sing, but he and Macko crossed their fingers that Branom would get through the set on the following day.

No such luck. After attempting "The Night" and a few other songs, Macko said Archer told Tim to take the whole day off, and to not talk, sing, or do anything with his voice. The members of Fifth Angel were worried. On the third day, they sent Branom home. Macko said Branom "blew out his voice." A few days after his departure, Branom said that the allergens and mold in Archer's basement impacted his voice. Whatever it was, with just three weeks away from their first-ever public performance, Fifth Angel once again did not have a singer.

McCormack remembers Branom pushing hard to get over the loudness of the band's instruments during rehearsal. The drummer recalled a full PA system being used in Archer's basement, along with Marshall stacks. It was high volume from the jump and that made it difficult for Branom to sing.

"Tim just couldn't keep up with it," McCormack said. "Up to that point, he was singing this retro 1960s music in Los Angeles. He had a great band called Cloud Nine. But he comes up here and tries to scream Fifth Angel heavy metal and he just wasn't there. His voice wasn't prepared, and he demolished himself in a rehearsal and a half."

Looking back on the situation in 2025, Branom admitted that a part of the reason it didn't work out for him and Fifth

Angel was that he wasn't ready to sing the material. Branom said he was working long hours for a record company at the time and couldn't devote the time necessary to get his voice in shape. That said, however, Branom was adamant that the environment Fifth Angel was rehearsing in was detrimental to his voice. He agreed with McCormack that everything was way too loud, and the singer was frustrated that Fifth Angel didn't spend the money to rent a rehearsal space.

"Some of the guys hadn't been in bands since the late-80s and Ed didn't want to go to a rehearsal place because he didn't want anyone hearing it, probably because he was a little nervous, even though there was nothing to be nervous about," Branom said. "A big part of my struggle was just how loud it was. It was too small of a room, they were too loud, and they tried to blame it on me. They wouldn't turn it down and I said, 'Just give me a couple of days and my voice will be right back,' but they didn't want to hear it."[25]

The band panicked and hoped Oliver Weinsheimer had enough time to find another group to take Fifth Angel's slot. But the promoter had other ideas. Macko said Weinsheimer was confident Fifth Angel could make the show happen.

"He said, 'No, John, I know you guys are going to come through and you're going to get a good singer,'" Macko recalled. "I was expecting him to just let us off the hook, and now we have got to go find a fucking singer in three weeks."

The members of Fifth Angel called everyone they knew

---

25. Branom provided this author with a video clip of him singing "Fifth Angel" with the band from the April 2010 rehearsals. Branom's tonal quality was very reminiscent of Ted Pilot. You could immediately tell Branom would have been an ideal fit with Fifth Angel.

and were open to suggestions. This author suggested asking Ronny Munroe, who was singing for Metal Church at the time. They tried to find former Heir Apparent singer Steve Benito. No one was available.

This book's author was at Fifth Angel's rehearsals following Branom's departure. After hearing me sing the entire 15-song set over Kendall Bechtel's monitor, they invited me up to sing a few songs, probably hoping to catch lightning in a bottle, as I knew all the lyrics to the songs. Sadly, since it was so loud in the basement and I had been singing as forcefully as I could for over an hour, my voice was in no shape to impress anyone. I sang "The Night," "Lights Out" and "We Rule." We had a great time, and the band loved having a voice as they rehearsed, but I clearly wasn't ready for prime time.

But the "newbie" in the band, Jeff McCormack, had an idea. Someone who sang with Heir Apparent back in 2006 at the same festival. Peter Orullian.

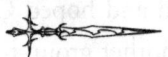

Peter Orullian was born on August 31, in Salt Lake City, Utah. He knew from a very young age that he could sing. One of Orullian's earliest memories is getting up on the piano bench to sing Christmas carols, which ultimately led to singing in church and at family parties.

By the time Peter was in high school, he started singing more formally, in the school choir. That expanded during Orullian's college years, as he started listening to hard rock and heavy metal and decided that he wanted to be in a band. Peter started looking in the newspapers, hoping to find rock groups advertising for a singer. He found one with Continuum.

After a couple of years, Continuum wanted to move into a bigger market, hoping to make a splash, and sign a record deal.

"We were one of the better bands in Salt Lake, and we wanted to make the leap," Orullian said. "I don't live there anymore, but at the time, Utah wasn't really a big music market. We talked about Los Angeles, but none of us really wanted to live there. At the time, Seattle had a lot of music industry activity because of the grunge scene, and we knew Queensrÿche was from there, plus a lot of other good metal bands, so we decided that's where we'd go."

Continuum recorded a handful of songs, and the future seemed promising. But the drummer of Continuum had a friend in Seattle who was a singer, and when the time came to move, Orullian had a sense he was going to be replaced. But while the drummer denied it, Peter knew it was going to happen (and it eventually did), and he made the move anyway, to work with Maestro David Kyle. Kyle lived on Alki Beach in Seattle and when he took Orullian as a student, it changed things for Peter immediately.

"He was amazing. I called him my own personal Yoda," Orullian said, referring to Kyle. "He'd make me stand at the piano looking out over Elliott Bay and tell me to throw my voice across it. He really taught me how to get a lot of volume and distance in my voice. … Of course, he taught scales and breathing, but the central technique was the mask, to sing into the mask, and really drilling that to make sure it was just natural and resonant."

Orullian took lessons from Maestro Kyle for a few years and then met a couple of musicians who were into similar music, namely the bands Rush, Yes, Dream Theater, and Queensrÿche. Orullian auditioned and got the gig. The band was called Inner Resonance.

Peter's union with Inner Resonance spawned an album, *Solar Voices*. It was released in 1999 by Descant Records. The website *progVisions* called the record a "promising debut," with "clean and shiny production" that could be enjoyed by fans of bands such as Shadow Gallery and Rush. Inner Resonance was deep into writing a follow-up album, but disbanded after guitarist Jeffrey Ryan Smoots encountered some health issues. Orullian took a breather from music after that.

Peter was working for Microsoft in the company's Entertainment and Devices division at this point. But in 2006, Heir Apparent guitarist Terry Gorle reached out to Orullian with an offer to sing for the band in Europe, including the Keep it True metal festival in Germany. Peter jumped at the chance. In November 2006, Orullian performed with Heir Apparent in Germany and then did two gigs in Greece—Athens and Thessaloniki. The band, which at the time included drummer Jeffrey McCormack, disbanded not long after the shows.

As Orullian tells it, he was sitting at home in April 2010 when Jeff called him and asked if he wanted to sing at the Keep it True festival again. Initially thinking it was for Heir Apparent, Peter said he would, but then Jeff mentioned it was for Fifth Angel.

"To be really honest, I had never heard of Fifth Angel," Orullian said. "Bad on me, I guess, but they went completely under my radar. Jeff said they needed somebody in two weeks, or they were going to cancel, so I said 'yes.' We did a handful of rehearsals over those two weeks, and I was trying to learn the material, as well as memorize all the lyrics."

Peter did a crash course on Fifth Angel's set, and the band was complete. But the group's long awaited live debut almost didn't happen. Ash from Iceland's erupting Eyjafjallajökull volcano was intense and created the highest level of air travel disruption since World War II. Several of the band members expressed concern that they would not be able to make the show. Fortunately, Fifth Angel's flight was cleared, and it was wheels up to Germany, for what would be a historic performance for the band.

"That was a very stressful Keep it True; luckily, we knew early [on] that the Fifth Angel flights were working … but I had to replace seven or eight bands during one or two days," Weinsheimer said. "It was horrible, and I did not sleep for at least two or three days. I hope it will never happen again, but we saved the show."

Fifth Angel made its live debut on April 24, 2010, at the Keep it True Festival in Lauda-Königshofen, Germany. The band members were received as true rock stars, and the reception Fifth Angel got from the crowd surprised everyone in the group.

"I watched the full show as it was their first show and one for the history books," Weinsheimer said. "The band sounded tight and great. The audience reactions were amazing, and the band was shocked that people could sing their songs. It was a complete success."

Orullian didn't have quite enough time to commit all the lyrics to memory, and referenced lyric sheets taped to the stage. But the crowd certainly didn't mind. Peter told the band at the outset that he and Ted Pilot are very different singers, but Orullian's performance of the songs from *Fifth Angel* and *Time Will Tell* was done with conviction, which went over well.

"I didn't actually make any effort to try and mimic Ted because I think that would have looked or sounded forced," Orullian said. "I much prefer when a vocalist just decides to sing a song with their natural voice and that's what I did."

Footage of Fifth Angel's debut live performance was uploaded to various social media platforms and shared liberally amongst fans. One of the people watching was Ken Mary.

"They did great without me, and I was really quite proud," Mary said. "Watching a crowd of 5,000 people singing along to songs like 'In the Fallout' and 'Fifth Angel' that we created that many years ago was crazy. We had no idea the impact that we had overseas until really that festival."

Mary was also supportive of the performances of McCormack and Orullian, adding that the two "did the family proud."

Returning home on a high, Fifth Angel was energized to continue and write new songs. But despite all the goodwill generated by Fifth Angel's appearance, the band wanted to go in a different direction, vocally. On September 15, 2010, in a statement issued through this author, Fifth Angel took to the internet to announce the band was looking for a permanent lead singer.

"We need someone [who] understands Fifth Angel is not going to be a gig where we hit the road without an end in sight," Archer said in the statement. "We all have a passion for music, and this band is the perfect way to express musical thoughts and ideas, while maintaining our lives that we've established. This is an opportunity for anyone interested to create new music, play some festivals and have some fun."

Orullian remembered not having any thought of being committed to Fifth Angel at the time. He considered the April 2010 show in Germany to be a one-off for him, and Orullian's career as an author was starting to take off.

"We really appreciate everything Peter did for us by

stepping in, learning our songs in a very short period of time and delivering a killer set at the Keep it True festival," Archer said in the statement. "Peter is an amazing creative talent, and his new book publishing deal will keep him busy. We all wish him the best of luck."

Fifth Angel set off to find a new voice, and they found one, at least briefly, in the middle of the Arizona desert.

David Fefolt was born on October 19, 1963, in Pittsburgh, Pennsylvania. He fronted a variety of hard rock and heavy metal bands from 1984-1991, including Valhalla and Forty Thieves. After a break from music, Fefolt was living in Arizona, and he sang for Angels of Babylon. The group, which also featured Megadeth bassist David Ellefson, and guitarist Ethan Brosh (who would later join Fifth Angel), put out *Kingdom of Evil* in 2010.

Fefolt flew to Seattle in 2010 to rehearse with Fifth Angel for the first time. The group convened at Evolution Studios in Bellevue, Washington. But it didn't work out quite as the band had hoped it would.

"David came up and we rented a rehearsal space and went through old Fifth Angel songs," Archer said. "I remember that it was ridiculously loud. We were too loud, and it was an issue as far as David being able to hear himself and sing loud enough. It was stupid of us to do that, and I don't remember why it ended up being that way."

Regardless, Fifth Angel felt good enough about the chemistry with Fefolt to move forward. The band named Fefolt as their singer on January 2, 2011, stating that they would release a new record later that year. Fefolt was also singing for the band FireWölfe at the time (and would appear on that group's self-titled album later in the year), and the plan was for Fefolt to front both bands. But as quickly as Fifth Angel came together, things fell apart again.

The band wanted to make a record and estimated it would require roughly $9,000-$10,000 to do it properly. McCormack booked three headline gigs for Fifth Angel that would have paid for the studio time. One was in Seattle, at the King Cat Theater, another was in Colorado, and the third was at Jaxx, in West Springfield, Virginia.

The drummer was able to negotiate $3,000 for each show for the band, along with travel expenses—quite a sum for a relatively unknown band who had only performed in public once. But Fifth Angel canceled all three times, before the concerts were even announced. This angered promoters, and the cancelations haunted the band in years to come.

Fefolt cut a few demos with Fifth Angel, including the tracks "End of Days," "World on Fire,"[26] and "Wicca." Archer described the songs as "works in-progress," that would have been modified significantly if the band had moved forward with them.

"As an example, 'World on Fire," has a slightly different melody than what the final version would have been," Archer said. "Some tunes have some audio effects, while other tracks do not that were supposed to."

Macko was frank in his assessment of the tunes, saying he wasn't impressed, and that Fefolt's vocals "just didn't have the right vibe." The bassist added that Nuclear Blast was interested in possibly signing Fifth Angel at the time, and the band sent

---

26. The demo of "World on Fire" has a running time of 9:23. Had the song been finished, it would have been the longest Fifth Angel song ever recorded.

a couple of Archer's early demos with Fefolt to the label for consideration. Nuclear Blast passed on the songs, telling the band that the tracks didn't sound like Fifth Angel to them.

"That really took the steam out of our first reunion," Macko said. "And Dave [Fefolt] was very stubborn, and everything was either his way or the highway and that didn't really go over too well with us."

McCormack, however, remembers things a bit differently. He called Fefolt a very good singer and writer, who ran up against old school songwriting and recording methods.

"Ed had written a bunch of songs, and he was pretty much dead set on those being the next Fifth Angel record," McCormack said. "God bless Ed, I love him to death, he's one of my favorite people, but he was very, 'This is going to be this way, and you're going to do this,' and David didn't like that. He didn't like that Ed was going to be in the booth with him and tell him how to sing. David wanted to be able to record stuff on his own and do this thing. And Ed was not interested in that."

Discussing Fefolt in 2025, Archer recalled thinking the singer had a cool voice, but like Orullian's, it was very different than Pilot's. Archer likened it to how different the voices are between David Lee Roth and Sammy Hagar when both had stints fronting Van Halen.

"I do remember conversations about whether he could sing the old stuff and if his voice was going to work," Archer said, regarding Fefolt. "If things had panned out with Fefolt, maybe it would have been like that sort of thing with [the Sammy Hagar era of] Van Halen, where there's the music with the new singer, and the old music, well, shit out of luck, except for a couple of songs, sorry."

Come summer 2011, Fifth Angel and Fefolt went their

separate ways. The rest of the band initially tried to continue working together. Archer described it as a period of false starts where things were always in a state of flux. Bechtel and McCormack came up with new song ideas, but the drummer said they kept either being shot down, or just not being worked on by Archer and Macko.

From Archer's perspective, 2011 brought a litany of personal changes which took up most of his time. Most importantly, Archer became the primary custodial parent of his son. With a busy schedule of juggling a non-musical career with full-time parenting, the band understandably fell lower on his priority list. In a nutshell, work on Fifth Angel music slowed.

Ultimately, McCormack had enough and quit. Fifth Angel went silent for another five years, with all the members going back to their own individual projects and lives. But come 2016, another festival invitation spurred Fifth Angel back to life once again.

Jeffrey McCormack during Fifth Angel's rehearsals for Keep it True in April 2010.
Photos courtesy of Tim Branom.

John Macko singing and laying down the bass groove during Fifth Angel's rehearsals for Keep it True in April 2010. Photo courtesy of Tim Branom.

A stage-used setlist from Fifth Angel's first-ever live performance on April 24, 2010, at the Keep it True Festival.

Fifth Angel relaxing in Germany in April 2010.
Photos courtesy of Ed Archer.

Peter Orullian warming up before Fifth Angel takes the stage in 2010. Photo by and courtesy of Michael "Paranoid" Hoenninger.

Peter Orullian performing with Fifth Angel on April 24, 2010, at the Keep it True Festival. Photo by and courtesy of Michael "Paranoid" Hoenninger.

Fifth Angel performing at the Keep it True Festival on April 24, 2010.
Photos by and courtesy of Michael "Paranoid" Hoenninger.

Autographed poster featuring the short-lived David Fefolt-fronted version of Fifth Angel. Circa 2010-2011.

"So take the hand of someone trusted and sail into the night."

- Fifth Angel, "We Will Rise"

Chapter 9
We Will Rise

In 2016, Oliver Weinsheimer invited Fifth Angel to perform at the Keep it True festival for a second time. The band agreed, and Fifth Angel was scheduled to play on April 29, 2017. And this time, original drummer Ken Mary planned to be with them.

"Ken actually played a big role in kick-starting things again in 2016," Archer said. "He called and was interested in doing something with Fifth Angel and wanted to be a part of it. Not only was he interested, but he was also instigating it. He was the motivating force behind us playing again."

With Pilot unavailable to front the band, Fifth Angel asked Peter Orullian to sing with them again, and he readily agreed. Fifth Angel also booked a warm-up gig for April 22, 2017, at El Corazón (formerly Graceland and the Off Ramp) in Seattle.

As the gig in Seattle approached, Fifth Angel was hit with what could have been devastating news. Ken Mary injured his shoulder while practicing and was not able to play with the band. Fifth Angel's old friend, and the only drummer to publicly play with the band up to that point, Jeff McCormack, came to Fifth Angel's rescue.

McCormack was also playing Keep it True with fellow

Seattle band Q5, and he was happy to fill in for Fifth Angel's shows as well. Ken felt horrible about not performing, and he believed it was the first time that he ever had to cancel a performance in his career.

"If I could have done it, I would've done it," Mary said. "I felt so bad. I felt bad for the band, but I did feel good knowing that Jeffrey would be able to step in and make it happen."

Just like they did in 2010, Fifth Angel practiced in Archer's basement to get ready for the two shows. Being well rehearsed, Orullian didn't need any lyric sheets on stage this time, and Fifth Angel was as prepared as they could be to present their music live.

A ticket from Fifth Angel's show on April 22, 2017, in Seattle, Washington. The gig was the band's first public performance in the United States.

Fifth Angel fans from all over the United States flew in to witness the band's show at El Corazón. Local music celebrities also came out. Jeff Loomis from Nevermore was in the crowd. People said they saw Mike McCready from Pearl Jam as well.

Some members of Fifth Angel remember the gig being a little shaky and not as well attended as they had hoped. But from a fan perspective, over the course of 80 minutes, Fifth Angel delivered a set that for all in attendance, was over 30 years in the making. Eight songs from *Fifth Angel* and seven from *Time Will Tell* were played, with the band closing the main set with "We Rule," and then an encore of their version of UFO's "Lights Out."

Unbeknownst to most people in the audience and the band members themselves, the gig was witnessed by one of their alumni. Original Fifth Angel vocalist Ted Pilot was in the crowd that night. Pilot kept his presence on the down-low, and wasn't spotted until the lights came up after the show.

"It was very strange to see someone else singing my stuff," Pilot said, recalling the show eight years later. "I kind of hung out in the back of the room but met Peter after the performance. He seemed to be a pretty cool guy. Much different tonal qualities, so I was wrapping my head around that. But I could hear the David Kyle influence though."

This author had the good fortune to introduce Pilot and Orullian after the gig. Orullian remembered the meeting and appreciated Pilot coming to the show.

"I was very flattered that he would come because some singers are weird about that," Orullian said. "They don't want to see a guy who is singing their stuff. But he was very gracious."

Despite the good vibes in the crowd, McCormack recalled Fifth Angel being "discouraged" afterward, due to a smaller than anticipated audience. The drummer wondered why there was no promotion for the gig, but ultimately, Fifth Angel's performance did what they intended it to do—serve as a dress rehearsal.

"This was our 'kick-the-tires' thing to see how things were going to go before we went to Germany, and there was no glitz or glam on stage," McCormack said. "It was just me sitting on a rug, and the rest of the guys around me. It worked out fine and we got the bugs out."

Archer didn't mind the smaller crowd. From his perspective, it was a cool opportunity to do a live rehearsal in front of people and get ready for Keep it True.

Stage-used kick drum head from Fifth Angel's performance at the Keep it True Festival on April 29, 2017. Signed by Jeffrey McCormack to the author.

"I didn't see it as disappointing," Archer said. "It was a warm-up gig. I thought it was successful and then we headed to Germany with more practice under our belts."

Keep it True was an exhilarating event for everyone in Fifth Angel. It was only the band's third live show, but with Orullian now rehearsed and familiar with the band's material, Fifth Angel delivered a tight and powerful live set for the crowd.

The quintet played the same 15 songs they performed at Keep at True seven years prior, but attendees were ecstatic to see them. As one fan who was in the front row put it, "After about 30 years, you still remember the words, as this music is timeless."

"I think the second Keep it True show was even better than the first one as the band was more confident in their abilities, and they knew what to expect," Weinsheimer said. "I was very proud of them growing as musicians."

Following Fifth Angel's lauded performance at Keep it True in 2017, the band was approached by Nuclear Blast A&R and Product Manager Jaap Wagemaker. Macko said Wagemaker gave him a business card, and told the bassist that the band sounded good, and they should make a record. While a partnership with the label did not work out several years prior, Fifth Angel was keen to write new music, and it was too good of an opportunity to pass up.

According to Orullian, Wagemaker showered the singer and Fifth Angel with praise after the show. The next morning, however, the excitement was dulled somewhat. Orullian recalled spotting Macko and his daughter having breakfast, and when the singer stopped to say hello, Macko was reserved about the interest shown by Nuclear Blast.

"John was kind of 'we'll wait and see' about the record label's excitement," Orullian said. "I don't know if that was because he'd been burned before or what."

When Fifth Angel finally got back stateside, they started writing songs. Archer had some riff ideas, as did Macko. Bechtel also came to the table with some songs, and the band fleshed out a few more tunes.

Recording scratch vocals for the songs was a problem though. Orullian didn't have a home studio at the time. The singer quickly invested in Pro Tools and became familiar with the technology. But as he began recording some vocal tracks, Orullian had reservations about the words he was asked to sing.

"I was reading them and thinking, 'This shouldn't be the band's next chapter of music lyrically,' so I rewrote the song with new lyrics that tied to building mythology around Fifth Angel, creating a deeper world and story," Orullian said. "I wrote a new melodic line to deliver it, and I recorded it all."

Orullian was up front with the band that he was not going to mimic Ted Pilot on new Fifth Angel songs. Orullian had his own vocal style that was (and is) reminiscent of James LaBrie (Dream Theater) and Geoff Tate (Queensrÿche). And ultimately, that did not sit well with the group.

Peter remembered having a band call with everyone in Fifth Angel, and the other members hemmed and hawed over Orullian's vocals.

"It was clear they were firing me, but kept talking around the issue," Orullian said. "Rather than just say they wanted a different sounding singer or wanted Fifth Angel to have lyrics that sounded more like the 1980s, they just kept talking in circles. I was the one who finally had to say, 'So, it sounds like you guys are firing me. I don't want to be in a band that doesn't want me. So, I wish you guys the best.'"

Fifth Angel severed ties with Orullian, which angered the singer, as he'd stepped up twice to bail the band out for live shows, made an investment in studio gear to record for them, and then started to write lyrics and melodies to try and help the band grow. It was the latter that Orullian felt likely got him axed.

"I don't think the guys appreciated that I was writing," Orullian said. "The impression I got was they didn't want to share songwriting credits; they just wanted me to sing what they wrote. It was good to get that figured out early, since that's not what I was interested in doing."

Archer didn't recall that being the case. He remembered the decision to part ways with Orullian had more to do with the singer's inexperience with Pro Tools and home recording (at the time). Regardless, Fifth Angel once again needed a singer. And this time, they looked from within to find the right voice for a new album.

Kendall Bechtel is known as an extraordinary guitar player. But his incredible talent as a singer had flown under the radar for most of his career. He was the lead singer on James Byrd's 1998 album, *Crimes of Virtuosity*, and had fronted various musical projects of his own over the years. This author even encouraged Kendall to sing lead during rehearsals for Fifth Angel's Keep It True performance in 2010. He declined at the time, but in 2017, Fifth Angel desperately needed someone to step up to the microphone. And Kendall Bechtel delivered.

With the group having an opportunity to potentially sign with Nuclear Blast, Bechtel whipped up a couple of demos and put his vocals on them. Once the tracks were approved by Mary and Macko, they sent them to Wagemaker, who, according to the band, loved what he heard.

Songwriting sessions commenced from summer 2017 through 2018, with Mary and Bechtel leading the charge. One of the early demos from Bechtel was "Nova Cain," which eventually turned into "We Will Rise." Archer stepped away from the band in late 2017 to handle some personal issues, which necessitated another writing collaboration to get the album done.

"It quickly became obvious that there was a partnership and a certain amount of magic between Ken and Kendall," Macko said. "They complement each other well."

Nuclear Blast signed Fifth Angel in May 2018, and the band finally had another record deal, nearly three decades after being dropped by Epic Records. In a statement announcing the signing, Wagemaker gushed about the songs Fifth Angel sent him, saying the music "captured the sound and the spirit of the old classics."

"The first three songs we gave them were 'Stars Are Falling,' 'We Will Rise,' and 'Queen of Thieves,' and they basically signed the band based on those three songs," Mary said. "We kind of knew we had something when we finished off those."

The group's first record for Nuclear Blast was *The Third Secret*, released on October 26, 2018. The album was produced by Ken Mary, recorded and engineered by Mary, Bechtel, Macko, Steve Conley, and Connor Hurley. *The Third Secret* was mastered by Brad Blackwood. Recorded primarily as a power trio, work took place at Mary's studio, SonicPhish Productions, and the home studios of Bechtel and Macko. The 10-track offering spans over 43 minutes, showcasing Fifth Angel's penchant for crafting aggressive metal classics and more cerebral, mid-tempo cuts.

"I love it and think it's an incredible work of art," Mary said. "I think it really is a beautiful album. It went together so quickly and easily. It was really stunning the way that just flowed out of us, and I think it's alive. That's what Kendall and I always talked about. There's life in the tracks and an emotion to it."

Although Macko was credited as a co-songwriter on four tracks, he said his major contribution was song arrangement.

"They cranked it out pretty quick," Macko recalled. "I had a couple ideas that I submitted that wound up on there. There's one song, 'Hearts of Stone,' that I wrote the music for, but it was really Kendall who took my idea and rewrote it."

Bechtel and Mary shaped the lyrics very much in line with Fifth Angel's first two albums. There are references to issues of faith and apocalyptic visions throughout the material.[27] *The Third Secret* features the artwork of Zsofia Dankova, who played off the themes from both the Shrapnel Records and Epic Records versions of Fifth Angel's first album. The fifth angel is depicted as a soldier of faith, with sweeping wings and a sword in-hand, ready to fight what emerges from a pit.

The guitar work on *The Third Secret* is passionate, showcasing Bechtel's skill as both a soloist and a rhythm player. Some of the guitarist's lead breaks have certain motifs that call back to his work on *Time Will Tell*, bringing familiarity to the material.

"We're all sort of hypercritical musicians when it comes down to it," Bechtel said. "So, this is a help and a hindrance sometimes. It's a delicate sort of fulcrum or threshold to deal with. Because without self-criticism, you're not going to get any better. ... The four of us, everyone who served in Fifth Angel, is multi-talented and kind of picky musicians."

As one would expect, Fifth Angel was enthusiastic about its new material. Nuclear Blast issued three songs as singles: "The Third Secret," "Can You Hear Me?" and "Stars Are Falling." The latter two had lyric videos made, but the title track received the full music video treatment.

By this time, Archer had returned to the band, and he appears in the video for "The Third Secret." While Archer did not play on the album, the guitarist was back in time to take part in promotional activities and was committed to

---

27. The lyrical content of *The Third Secret* is influenced by a series of prophecies called the *Three Secrets of Fátima*.

supporting Fifth Angel's new music. One of his favorites on *The Third Secret* is "Fatima."

"That's a standout to me, it's a really cool vibe and feeling with that tune," Archer said.

Talking about *The Third Secret* before its release, Archer said it was critical for Fifth Angel to revisit the band's past work. Specifically, the group wanted songs that examined the direction of humanity and helped expand the lyrical content found on *Fifth Angel* and *Time Will Tell*.

Mary agreed, noting that people who loved songs such as "The Night" and "Seven Hours" should find something to enjoy on *The Third Secret*.

"I think we really poured our hearts into the record, and we tried to do something collectively ... [that] we were excited about," Mary said.

"We hope the fans will hear the classic threads of the Fifth Angel they know and love, along with the growth and maturity the individuals of the band have gone through over the years," Bechtel said in a statement when *The Third Secret* was released. "We hope they love the new songs as much as we do!"

Archer gave Bechtel a ton of credit for his work on *The Third Secret*, noting how his bandmate had flourished as a songwriter, guitarist and vocalist over the years.

"Kendall was really wanting to be more involved in the creative process, as he wasn't part of the first Fifth Angel record and just played leads on *Time Will Tell*," Archer said. "I heard Kendall sing on his own stuff, and his approach is a bit different than what he used on *The Third Secret*. I liked it and thought it was cool. It served the music and album well. I thought Kendall did a really good job."

Reviews of *The Third Secret* were overwhelmingly positive.

Chris Hawkins, writing for *Antihero* said, "The guitar sound is so vividly alive, radiating in sparkling distorted splendor, though viciously violent as well, a monster plated with metal." Mark Diggins with *The Rockpit* called *The Third Secret* "classic rock/metal at its very best and the most incredible thing of all is that there's not a song on here that won't grab your full attention." Rodrigo Altaf of *Sonic Perspectives* gave the album an 8/10 rating, saying *The Third Secret* "preserves the DNA of what made Fifth Angel what they were in the 80s, and adds an extra dose of heaviness."

The band was thrilled by how well *The Third Secret* was received by fans and critics. At the start of the promotional cycle for the album, Fifth Angel had some trepidation about how much time had lapsed and what people would think of the group's evolution.

"We were nervous about it and very concerned," Mary admitted. "We knew the first two albums were considered classics in Europe, and you're fighting, at that point, nostalgia, which is a very powerful force. And so, we were like, 'How are we going to make a record that people will not immediately hate because it's different?' It's going to be different, 28 years later. But somehow, I think we really were successful in making music that still sounded like Fifth Angel, it was still exciting, and still moved us, and was still exciting to us. I think that's why it was received very well."

With the record out and festival offers rolling in, Fifth Angel needed to figure out how to present the music live. Bechtel was up to the challenge of singing the songs from *The Third Secret*, but he wanted another singer to do the material from *Fifth Angel* and *Time Will Tell*. As it turns out, the guy for the job was nearly in Ken Mary's backyard.

Fifth Angel's *The Third Secret* was released on October 26, 2018. It was the group's first new album in nearly 30 years.

Promotional imagery used by Nuclear Blast to market *The Third Secret*.

Fifth Angel performs at the Keep it True Festival on April 29, 2017. Photo by and courtesy of Michael "Paranoid" Hoenninger.

Ed Archer and Peter Orullian performing at the Keep it True Festival on April 29, 2017. Photo by and courtesy of Michael "Paranoid" Hoenninger.

Jeffrey McCormack performs at the Keep it True Festival on April 29, 2017. Photo by and courtesy of Michael "Paranoid" Hoenninger.

John Macko and Kendall Bechtel perform at the Keep it True Festival on April 29, 2017. Photo by and courtesy of Michael "Paranoid" Hoenninger.

John Macko and Jeffrey McCormack perform at the Keep it True Festival on April 29, 2017. Photo by and courtesy of Michael "Paranoid" Hoenninger.

Fifth Angel stands triumphant after concluding their performance at the Keep it True Festival on April 29, 2017. Photo by and courtesy of Michael "Paranoid" Hoenninger.

Kendall Bechtel performing on April 22, 2017, at El Corazón, in Seattle, Washington. Photo by and courtesy of Bobby Ferkovich.

Peter Orullian performing on April 22, 2017, at El Corazón, in Seattle, Washington. Photo by and courtesy of Bobby Ferkovich.

Ed Archer (left) and John Macko (right) delivering the goods, Fifth Angel-style, on April 22, 2017, at El Corazón, in Seattle, Washington.
Photos by and courtesy of Bobby Ferkovich.

Peter Orullian and Kendall Bechtel unite for a vocal harmony on April 22, 2017, at El Corazón, in Seattle, Washington. Photo by and courtesy of Bobby Ferkovich.

John Macko (left), Peter Orullian (center) and Ed Archer (right) during an atmospheric moment in Fifth Angel's performance on April 22, 2017, at El Corazón, in Seattle, Washington. Photo by and courtesy of Bobby Ferkovich.

From the Congregation

Fifth Angel Plays Its First U.S. Show in Seattle

By James R. Beach[28]

I've been a fan of Fifth Angel since 1987, when I purchased a slightly used copy of the original 1986 Shrapnel release. All these years later, I'm not sure if I heard about them from a friend, read about them in *The Rocket* or some other music publication, or just liked the cover art and the band shot on the back. But I do know I loved it when I got home and put it on the turntable.

I bought the reissue of the debut, and the follow-up album, *Time Will Tell*, when those came out on Epic Records as well, and anticipating seeing them live sometime soon. Sadly, despite being on a major label and other labelmates such as Sanctuary and Riot out touring, Fifth Angel never hit the road. Before long, Fifth Angel split-up and I figured that was that. Another great band that never got out of the Pacific Northwest and simply fizzled out.

Fast forward to 2016, and I was working on a big

---

28. James R. Beach is co-owner of Northwest Metalworx Music, an independent record label that specializes in unearthing lost Pacific Northwest hard rock and heavy metal music. He is also the primary author of *Rusted Metal, Building an Empire: The Story of Queensrÿche, and Beyond the Black: The Story of Metal Church*.

reference guide on heavy metal and hard rock bands and music in the Pacific Northwest called *Rusted Metal*. I was fortunate to be able to land an interview with original Fifth Angel guitarist James Byrd for the book, as well as chat with newer drummer Jeffrey McCormack (who played with Fifth Angel for their first public live performance in 2010 in Europe and was preparing to do it again at that time). Additionally, one of my co-writers, Jim Sutton, also interviewed Fifth Angel guitarist Ed Archer. Shortly afterward, Fifth Angel announced a warm-up show for its 2017 performance at Keep it True in Germany. And thankfully, it was booked at El Corazón in Seattle.

    The concert was something I never thought I would ever get to see, and I was super excited to make the trip up for it. The lineup consisted of McCormack on drums, *Time Will Tell*-era guitarist Kendall Bechtel, Archer on second guitar, bassist John Macko and singer Peter Orullian, who had fronted the band in 2010. The show was awesome, and Fifth Angel played tracks from both of their studio albums from the 1980s. As a bonus, original singer Ted Pilot came to watch the show, and I had a chance to meet him and chat for a bit as well. I still have my T-shirt from the concert which features the cover art from the Epic version of Fifth Angel's debut album.

    Since then, Fifth Angel has released two more albums, *The Third Secret* and *When Angels Kill*, which I bought when they came out. I think they are both killer and continue the legacy of this great band.

Chapter 10
Angels of Mercy

Steven Carlson was born in San Diego, California. He started his music career as a drummer and singer in various bands, and he was influenced by groups such as Slade, Nazareth, Deep Purple and Black Sabbath. Carlson moved to Seattle in the early 1980s when he was in his twenties.

At that time, he was in a band called Twisted Sister (no, not the one you are thinking of), which played shows throughout the Pacific Northwest. Twisted Sister played five or six nights a week, complete with a full stage production, including its own PA system and stage lighting.

Carlson also played with Redax, out of Renton, Washington. Carlson would switch off with the band's regular drummer and play five or six songs. Brett Miller, a native of Bellevue, Washington, and the bassist of Lipstick, vividly remembers Carlson's days in Redax.

"They did a good version of U2's 'New Year's Day,'" Miller said. When Steve sang the line, "The newspaper says, says, Say it's true,' he would pull out a copy of *The Seattle Times* rolled up out of his back pocket as a prop."

Like many musicians in Seattle at the time, Carlson was in multiple bands concurrently to make ends meet. He also fronted The Machine, the band John Macko played bass in at one point. But the two musicians were never in the group at the same time. Eventually, after spending decades in the Seattle area, Carlson moved to Phoenix, Arizona, in 1997.

"I didn't know what I was going to do then," Carlson said. "I wasn't thinking about playing music, but then I started playing in a few tribute bands."

Carlson became the vocalist of The Crüe, a tribute to Mötley Crüe, and he also played drums for Heart to Heart, a tribute band honoring Seattle rock icons Heart. But original music was on the horizon for Carlson. In November 2014, Carlson and three other musicians formed Color of Chaos, a hard rock band performing out of Phoenix. Since then, Color of Chaos has opened for some international stars, including Megadeth, Y&T, and Dokken. But it was Color of Chaos' very first show, opening for Steel Panther, on February 13, 2016, at Livewire AZ in Scottsdale, Arizona, that set the wheels in motion for Carlson to front Fifth Angel.

Mike Gaube, a disc jockey/concert promoter/booking agent in Arizona, became a big fan of Color of Chaos and Carlson, as a singer. Unbeknownst to Carlson at the time, Gaube also was a huge fan of Fifth Angel, and well connected in the Arizona rock scene, including knowing Ken Mary. This would prove fortuitous shortly.

On November 12, 2017, Carlson and his family went to a drum clinic held by Ken Mary in Cave Creek, Arizona. After it was over, Steven and Ken talked, and the former mentioned a mutual connection with Fifth Angel bassist John Macko. About six months later, Fifth Angel got an offer to play a festival in early 2019. And then Carlson got the call to sing with the band.

"They asked Mike Gaube if he knew anybody, and he offered my name up," Carlson said. "From there, I came in and did a couple of demos with Ken at his studio. He sent it out to the band and Kendall really liked it. They liked what I could bring to the band."

Gaube remembered Ken Mary asking him if he knew anyone who could sing for Fifth Angel. Without hesitation, Gaube sent Mary a video of Carlson singing live with Color of Chaos. Needless to say, it went over well.

"Getting Steve in the band was my recommendation, and I'm pretty proud of that," Gaube said. "I had to think for a few seconds in my head when Ken asked me, but Steve was the one. There were two or three guys that came to mind, but he was top of the list."[29]

Little did Carlson know, just a few months later, he would be the *only* lead vocalist in Fifth Angel.

With another singer on board, a new album getting positive press, and shows booked, 2019 was shaping up to be a banner year for Fifth Angel. But just as Fifth Angel was taking off, the bottom dropped out—again.

Bechtel had just come off a tour performing with fellow Seattle-based hard rock band Q5. The experience did not go well and allegedly caused the guitarist to have second thoughts about gigging with Fifth Angel in Europe.

"Staying in weird hotels with guys and rooming together, he just didn't want to go through that experience that you have when you're a beginning artist," Carlson said, who had formed a close bond with Bechtel by fall 2018. "It's a rough scene and I think he felt like, 'I don't want to do this anymore.'"

---

29. Gaube said James Rivera (Helstar, Vicious Rumors) was one of the other vocalists Fifth Angel considered.

Mary agreed, but thought the timing was suspect.

"It was a little weird because the album came out and then he's like, 'I don't want to tour,' and I'm like, 'Well, that's a problem, we need to play some shows,'" Mary said. "Why do you go through the process of doing a record and signing with a label and doing all these things and then just not want to tour?"

From Macko's perspective, he felt the tension with Kendall had been building since the recording sessions for *The Third Secret*.

"Ken would ask him for tracks and Kendall wouldn't send them, or he wouldn't send him the right tracks," Macko said. "There was a point where Ken was so mad, he goes, 'I'll just finish the whole rest of the record without Kendall.' I had to step in and be the mediator to get both guys working together. That happened. That's when this odd behavior really started rearing its ugly head with Kendall."

By December 2018, as Fifth Angel was discussing its touring plans for the upcoming year, Bechtel was done with the band.

"We were having a discussion about one of the festivals, I think it was the Rock Hard festival, and there was something about the deal he didn't like," Macko said, regarding Bechtel. "He flew off the handle. We were having a group call, and he started yelling and then he just hung up."

Archer called it a "miscommunication" between all of them. The guitarist remembers discussions about doing some warm-up shows in Arizona (where Mary and Carlson live), and one gig in particular set Bechtel off.

"One of the things that came up was a free show, not free to the band, but free to the public, our expenses would have been paid, and it was a promotional show for people who wanted to check us out," Archer said. "Someone might have posted about the show publicly, and I think there was a misunderstanding with Kendall's interpretation of this whole thing, and things got heated in discussions and it escalated and snowballed out of control fairly quickly. Before I knew it, it sounded like Kendall didn't want to participate in anything. I was watching things unfold through emails and text messages."

In retrospect, Macko said the business-like manner that he and Mary took regarding Fifth Angel at the time may have contributed to Bechtel's abrupt departure. Macko added that Bechtel is very much an artist, and in some instances, the business aspects of Fifth Angel frustrated the guitarist.

Despite the void left by Bechtel, Fifth Angel had things covered in the vocal department for its live dates in 2019, thanks to Steven Carlson. The veteran frontman had no trouble picking up the slack and singing the band's entire catalog.

"My job, at the time, was to emulate Ted [Pilot] as best as I could, and still be me," Carlson said. "And bring that energy, and bring more, if possible, energy to it. I didn't find out that I was going to do the songs from *The Third Secret* until like a month before."

With the vocalist issue settled, Fifth Angel turned its attention to the vacant lead guitarist spot. And with just weeks before Fifth Angel's performance at the Metal Assault Festival, they were scrambling to find someone who could competently play the guitar parts of Byrd and Bechtel.

This author suggested a young British guitarist named Alex Ward to Macko and Archer. Ward dutifully sent in videos of him playing Fifth Angel's songs. While Ward played well, the band wanted someone who was stateside. About the same time, former Megadeth bassist Dave Ellefson tipped Ken Mary to a guitar virtuoso named Ethan Brosh.

Ethan Brosh was born in the late 1970s, just outside New York City, in Suffern, New York. But the Brosh family moved to Israel when Ethan was very young, and that is where his musical journey truly began.

Classical music, not rock, is what first caught Ethan's ear. He took piano lessons and focused on the composers who moved him, particularly Johann Sebastian Bach. But what ignited his love of heavier music was art—specifically Iron Maiden T-shirts. As Brosh explained, he thought the band's mascot, Eddie, was cool, and kept buying shirts with him on them. He had no idea what the band sounded like until friends encouraged him to listen to Iron Maiden's music. Ethan discovered his brother had a cassette of Iron Maiden's *The Number of the Beast*, put it on, and was blown away by what he heard.

"I still picture me being at my neighbor's condo and us as kids—he was even younger than me, saying, 'Oh, that's all electric guitars,' and it was like just a switch flipped in my brain and I'm like, 'I think I know what I need to be doing for the rest of my life,'" Brosh said. "I started obsessing about getting an electric guitar."

Becoming the next Adrian Smith or Dave Murray took a while. Ethan's parents took education very seriously, and they believed their son should first learn how to play classical guitar. So, that's what Ethan did. But when he got his first electric guitar around age 12, Ethan started studying under Israeli guitarist Eyal Freeman. That instruction helped Brosh bloom as a guitar player, and he moved back to the United

States in May 2001 to study at Berklee College of Music, in Boston.

After graduating from Berklee, Ethan formed a hard rock band called Burning Heat. But the guitarist was finding his way as a solo artist as well. Mike Varney, in addition to founding Shrapnel Records, was now a part-owner of Magna Carta Records. His company released Brosh's first instrumental album, *Out of Oblivion*, in 2009. That record featured guest performances by George Lynch (Dokken) and Mike Mangini (Extreme, Dream Theater). The cover art was designed by Derek Riggs, who painted many of the Iron Maiden covers that Brosh loved as a kid.

Since then, Brosh has played guitar with Angels of Babylon (featuring David Ellefson of Megadeth), and cut several more solo records. Brosh and his solo band also opened for Yngwie Malmsteen, and later, Red Dragon Cartel, featuring another of Brosh's idols, Jake E. Lee.

Brosh became a fan of Fifth Angel in the late 1990s, while still living in Israel. He was listening to internet radio when the DJ introduced the band and Brosh wrote down the group's name. But when he finally bought one of Fifth Angel's records what he heard was a total surprise.

"I ordered the first album, and then when I got it, I was really disappointed because it did not sound at all like the song that I had heard," Brosh said. "Later on, I realized that all the cool stuff that appealed to me was on *Time Will Tell*."

Ken Mary phoned Ethan in January 2019 with an offer to play with Fifth Angel. But Brosh missed the call, and as the guitarist explained, letting the call from Ken go to voicemail was fortuitous.

"You either love it or hate it, but for the last 15 years I have a voicemail [greeting] that is a really long guitar solo," Brosh said. "Ken heard it and loved it, and left me a message saying something like, 'Man, I'm not sure if I got the right guy or whatever, but that solo sounded sick and not sure what you have going on, but in a month, we have this show in Germany, and my high school band, Fifth Angel, is in need of a guitar player.'"

Brosh was up to the task. The guitarist made his debut with Fifth Angel on February 16, 2019, at the Metal Assault Festival, at Posthalle, in Würzburg, Germany.

Fifth Angel played almost the entirety of its debut album on that night (only "Fade to Flames" was not performed), and three songs from *The Third Secret* ("Can You Hear Me?", "Stars Are Falling" and "The Third Secret"). But it was the five selections from *Time Will Tell* that excited Brosh the most. The guitarist explained that he connects with Bechtel's phrasing and style more than he does with Byrd's.

"I love 'Cathedral,' 'Midnight Love,' and 'Time Will Tell,'" Brosh said. "Anything on the second record I really enjoy. It has great guitar work and hooks, and I enjoyed doing the background vocals on some of those songs."

Fifth Angel made an announcement regarding its major lineup change on February 4, 2019, and played a total of three shows during the year. As it turns out, those were their only promotional dates in support of *The Third Secret*. The band performed "Dust to Dust" for the first time on June 9, 2019, at the Rock Hard Festival in Germany. A couple of months later, Fifth Angel did a short set at the Alcatraz Metal Festival in Belgium and then shut things down for the remainder of the year.

Reminiscing about Fifth Angel's trio of shows in support

of *The Third Secret*, Archer said he was blown away by Carlson's voice and stage presence fronting the band.

"It feels great, he is the best fit ever, we're so lucky to have him," Archer said. "Steve is a cool guy, he's funny, and there are certain elements of his personality that remind me of Ted. He's kind of a jokester the way Ted is. Steve is fun to travel with, and a great showman with a wonderful voice that has fire, emotion and grit. As Terry Brown would say, Steve has this je ne sais quoi with his voice. It's there, and it works."[30]

Mary was encouraged by Brosh's ability to step in for Fifth Angel on such short notice in 2019. He said Ethan was faced with a very difficult situation, not just filling in for one great guitar player in Byrd, but another in Bechtel.

"I think Ethan did really well, although it took him a little while to get his bearings," Mary said. "The more time that went by, he was getting better and growing into the role."

Unbeknownst to Fifth Angel, their Belgian gig would be the last time the band would take the stage again until 2023. Like everyone around the world, the COVID-19 pandemic and resulting shutdown threw a wrench into Fifth Angel's plans to support *The Third Secret*.

"COVID really just stopped the ball rolling, because the album had a very good reaction," Macko said. "We did those festivals that were very successful, and we were going to do some real touring in 2020."

Despite the pandemic, in September 2021, *The Third Secret* entered the German and Switzerland music charts at number 48 and number 51, respectively, showing the staying power the album had. Nuclear Blast's head of promotion,

---

30. *Je ne sais quoi* means an appealing quality that is not easily described.

Markus Wosgien, was thrilled at the chart positions the album achieved.

"Such an amazing result for this even more amazing record," Wosgien said. "Who has ever expected that they will even top their two legendary 80s milestones, with their first album after three decades? What a masterpiece, I truly love it!"

Nuclear Blast also reported that *The Third Secret* reached number 1 on soundcheck reviews from the news outlets/websites *Rock Hard*, *Rock It!* and *Powermetal.de*, along with taking the number two spot on *Deaf Forever* and *Metal.de*.

Looking to capitalize on the success of *The Third Secret*, Fifth Angel began writing for its next album. And Ken Mary had a lofty goal for it.

Promotional imagery for Fifth Angel's headline appearance at the Metal Assault Festival on February 16, 2019, in Würzburg, Germany.

Promotional image used by Nuclear Blast to announce the chart positions of Fifth Angel's *The Third Secret* and thank the fans.

Steven Carlson and John Macko performing on June 9, 2019, at the Rock Hard Festival in Germany.

1. THE NIGHT
2. CATHEDRAL
3. SEVEN HOURS
(TALK TO CROWD)
4. STARS ARE FALLING
(TALK TO CROWD)
5. CAN YOU HEAR ME?
6. CALL OUT THE WARNING
7. FIFTH ANGEL
(DRUM SOLO)
8. THE THIRD SECRET
9. MIDNIGHT LOVE   NO CLICK
10. TIME WILL TELL
11. WINGS OF DESTINY
(TALK TO CROWD)
12. IN THE FALLOUT
13. SHOUT IT OUT
14. CRY OUT THE FOOLS
15. WE RULE   BIG ENDING
(ENCORE)
16. LIGHTS OUT

Fifth Angel's setlist from the Metal Assault Festival on February 16, 2019, in Würzburg, Germany. Image courtesy of Michael "Paranoid" Hoenninger.

John Macko and Ethan Brosh performing on February 16, 2019, at the Metal Assault Festival in Würzburg, Germany. Photo by and courtesy of Michael "Paranoid" Hoenninger.

Steven Carlson performing on February 16, 2019, at the Metal Assault Festival in Würzburg, Germany. Photo by and courtesy of Michael "Paranoid" Hoenninger.

John Macko performing on February 16, 2019, at the Metal Assault Festival in Würzburg, Germany. Photo by and courtesy of Michael "Paranoid" Hoenninger.

Ken Mary performing on February 16, 2019, at the Metal Assault Festival in Würzburg, Germany. Photo by and courtesy of Michael "Paranoid" Hoenninger.

Ed Archer performing on February 16, 2019, at the Metal Assault Festival in Würzburg, Germany. Photo by and courtesy of Michael "Paranoid" Hoenninger.

Ethan Brosh in the middle of a guitar solo during Fifth Angel's performance at the Metal Assault Festival in Würzburg, Germany. Photo by and courtesy of Michael "Paranoid" Hoenninger.

Fifth Angel performing on February 16, 2019, at the Metal Assault Festival in Würzburg, Germany. Photo by and courtesy of Michael "Paranoid" Hoenninger.

Fifth Angel poses with photographer and heavy metal fan Michael "Paranoid" Hoenninger on February 16, 2019, at the Metal Assault Festival in Würzburg, Germany. Photo courtesy of Michael "Paranoid" Hoenninger.

From the Congregation

Shouting it Out Over the Airwaves

By Mike Gaube[31]

I became a fan of Fifth Angel after seeing an ad in one of the heavy metal magazines back in the 1980s. I saw that Ken Mary was the drummer, and the way he plays, he had become one of my favorite drummers. I remember him being on Chastain's *Ruler of the Wasteland*. So, I checked out the first Fifth Angel album because of all that and I liked it. So, when *Time Will Tell* came out, I was already a fan, and I loved it. But I was relieved when I found out Ken Mary was still drumming on the record, after not seeing him on the back cover.

But then Fifth Angel disappeared. The internet wasn't around back then, so you couldn't research anything. Years went by, and I got on the air at 93.3 KDKB in Phoenix, Arizona, and got my own show. It was originally called *Headbanger's Heaven* and it was a 7 p.m. to midnight show every Saturday night, so five hours of hard rock, metal and interviews. Some guy made a claim to the

---

31. Mike Gaube is a DJ and radio personality with KPKY (94.9 and 104.5—The Pick), broadcasting out of his hometown, Idaho Falls, Idaho. He's the host of *Mike Gaube's Headbangers* every Friday night. He is also a concert promoter and booker in Arizona, where he now makes his home.

show's name, so we changed the name. But as part of my show, I liked to bring on musicians and bands that have disappeared, and Ken Mary was one I thought of. Around 2008-2009, I emailed Ken at his studio (I *think*, ha, ha), SonicPhish Productions, and asked him to be on my show. He came down to the station, and we hung out and became friends.

I stayed in touch with Ken, and as I got more involved in the local music scene as a promoter, I had a lot of opportunities to have guys like George Lynch (Dokken, Lynch Mob), Frank Hannon (Tesla), Carlos Cavazo (Quiet Riot), Miljenko (Mili) Matijevic (Steelheart), Oni Logan (Lynch Mob) and Dwain Miller (Keel), come down and jam at my Headbanger's Bar Party. I think it was the first anniversary party, I invited Ken down to jam with George, and another guitarist, Steve Conley, who is now bandmates with Ken in Flotsam and Jetsam. That was the first time Ken had played live in quite some time. He thanked me for getting him back on stage, so I was happy to be a facilitator for that.

Several years went by, and when Ken was back with Fifth Angel and working on *The Third Secret*, he reached out to me in 2018 to help promote the band's new record and interview them at his studio. Nuclear Blast wanted to issue a few "trailer" videos leading up to the album's release. We had established a good relationship over the years, and as one of Fifth Angel's original fans from back in the day, helping launch the band's comeback record was a great opportunity. I was honored and excited, but nervous at the same time as the interview was being recorded. I've always been a fan, first and foremost. But I had no reason to be nervous.

I found out that Ed Archer is friendly, but quiet and reserved, John Macko can talk your ear off and is very friendly. And Kendall Bechtel, I see him as this mad scientist guitar player. I was always so impressed with his guitar playing, like his phrasing and even his pick attack, and to watch him in the studio was incredible. I remember Kendall just sitting there and he started doing the acoustic intro to "Broken Dreams," and he was like 'Ed, your turn," which I thought was funny, because Ed didn't even have a guitar in his hand. Kendall played the intro to "Midnight Love," which is a big favorite of mine, and then Ken started playing "We Will Rise" over the studio monitor and Kendall played live along with it. And it was really cool because he played two parts slightly different than what the recorded solo was. The guy didn't even warm up and was ripping off some killer stuff. In fact, off the cuff, and pretty much note for note, he blasted out "Eruption" by Van Halen.

Even though I heard some of Fifth Angel's new songs when I interviewed them, I didn't get to hear *The Third Secret* in its entirety until a few weeks before it came out. I went to Ken's studio to pick up a promotional copy of the record, and we went to lunch, and he played it in the car for me. "Stars Are Falling" came on, and I was like "Holy shit, that is bad ass," and now it's one of my favorite Fifth Angel songs. When Kendall's vocal comes in, it just blows me away.

Ken Mary is not only a great player, but he's incredible

in the studio. I love how he produces; he makes records like what I grew up with. What he produces just sounds good. He brings the best out of people. He made Kendall sound amazing. If you listen to some of Kendall's solo songs on YouTube, and then what he did on *The Third Secret*, Ken Mary pulled some balls out of him. Kendall sounded Dio-esque! What a performance!

When Fifth Angel was ready to play shows after *The Third Secret* was finished, Ken asked me if I knew any singers, as Kendall didn't want to tackle the material from the first two Fifth Angel albums. I suggested Steve Carlson, who is in a local band called Color of Chaos. Fifth Angel really liked him and when Kendall ultimately left the band, Steve stepped up and he's now Fifth Angel's lead singer and recorded all the vocals on the band's latest album, *When Angels Kill*. I'm proud to have played a small part in making that connection happen.

Chapter 11
LIGHT THE SKIES

As the world's population surfaced after the COVID-19 pandemic, Fifth Angel began writing its next album. With Bechtel no longer in the band, and two new people in the creative fold, the project started as a group effort. But the process was spearheaded by Ken Mary, who would ultimately serve as producer of the new record. The drummer's initial vision was to have every person who had ever been in Fifth Angel contribute to the album in some way.

By giving fans new music featuring spot playing/singing from Fifth Angel alumni, the new record would be definitively classic, yet modern enough to keep its integrity. Regrettably, while the plan sounded good in concept, not everyone was willing or able to commit.

"We contacted Ted, I contacted James, personally, and we reached out to Kendall. Nobody wanted to take part in this," Mary said. "Actually, I think Kendall, at one point later, I think he did agree to do some stuff, but we ran out of time. It would have been cool for the fans, so it's unfortunate."

Macko admitted he was disappointed in the lack of interest shown by his former bandmates.

"When you have a gift like that, I don't understand just throwing it away," Macko said. "Even though I stepped away from music for over 10 years, it still came back, caught up with me, and I got the itch. I felt like you can take the man out of the music, but you can't take the music out of the man."

Instead of letting the rejections derail things, Ken leaned into his own ideas, and those of Macko, Archer and Brosh. Slowly, but surely, a new Fifth Angel album started taking shape. Archer, who had not been part of the creative process on *The Third Secret*, had a few riffs and started working on songs. But as luck would have it, family health issues prevented the guitarist from being as involved with the new recording as he would have liked.

Macko felt horribly for Archer but also saw the situation as an opportunity to have his songs play a more prominent role in Fifth Angel's history.

"Ken has always been the biggest supporter of my writing," the bassist said. "He thinks I'm a great songwriter and has always pushed my ideas. It was good that I was able to fill in creatively in Ed's place."

Mary and Macko grabbed the creative reins for Fifth Angel and got to work. With Archer only a sporadic part of the songwriting process, Mary (who Macko says primarily composes on a keyboard) needed a foil to help translate his songs to guitar. And he found one in his friend and bandmate in Flotsam and Jetsam—guitarist Steve Conley.

Steve Conley has been a guitarist in Flotsam and Jetsam since 2013, when he took over for Edward Carlson. Conley played with ex-Megadeth bassist Dave Ellefson from 2004-2010 in a band called F5 and is a guitar teacher and songwriter. Conley lives in the greater Phoenix area and has been bandmates with Ken Mary since the latter joined Flotsam and Jetsam in 2018.

Conley stepped up to the plate in a big way as Fifth Angel was preparing its fourth album, which would eventually be titled *When Angels Kill*. In addition to bringing Mary's keyboard-written ideas to life on guitar, Conley co-wrote three tracks ("Resist the Tyrant," "We Are Immortal," and "Seven Angels"). In addition, Conley recorded a significant amount of rhythm guitar on the record.

Despite Brosh being credited as a co-writer on the title track and "Blinded and Bleeding," and serving as Fifth Angel's lead guitar player on stage, he did not play any guitar solos on *When Angels Kill*. There was some creative tension between Brosh, Macko, and Mary that almost led to Brosh's exit from the band.

Brosh explained that he and Ken Mary first completed the song "When Angels Kill." But the guitarist said there was a different song that Ken liked, so the drummer changed the lyrics and used the melody from the original song idea that Brosh had worked on with him. The guitarist added that his riffs got lifted and changed, and what was at first more of a showcase song for him ended up being the opposite. But the issues between Brosh and Fifth Angel really surfaced when it came time to lay down guitar solos.

"I started sending different solos and Ken loved everything that I played up until John came into the picture and started commenting about my solos just being 'okay' and if I could sound more like the first album and neo-classical in style," Brosh said. "I pushed back on that because the idea at first was Ken and Ed wanted my style of guitar playing to be all over this record. Once John started commenting, at one point, I said, 'Fine, I'll start doing some more neo-classical soloing,' and started sending things over and not really hearing anything back. ... A few months later, I find out the whole record is done, and the songs I co-wrote with Ken that he used, he finished himself."

Brosh went on to say that his guitar riffs were not played in the manner he intended. Guitarist Jim Dofka recorded all the guitar solos for the songs on *When Angels Kill*.[32] When asked about the issues with Brosh, Mary said that Ethan was more of a rock player in the sense of Eddie Van Halen as opposed to a neo-classical player and that Brosh simply did not like the direction Fifth Angel wanted to take on the album.

Macko agreed and said that the band collectively wanted to go back to the neo-classical guitar style on the first Fifth Angel record, and that Brosh did not compose solos that fit the vision he and Ken had. Eventually, Brosh and Fifth Angel put their differences aside. But as of this writing, the guitarist says he still does not have his own copy of *When Angels Kill* and improvises the guitar solos when performing the songs from the album.

Ken Mary wrote the lion's share of the lyrics for *When Angels Kill*, with Steven Carlson also contributing. Lyrically, the record is a conceptual work that weaves the themes and lyrics from Fifth Angel's first three records into a narrative. The story begins in the future, when a man named Phoenix realizes the current global leader must be stopped and joins a band of freedom fighters. Mary explained that the idea was to give fans something that they could dig into, with callbacks that send listeners back to Fifth Angel's previous albums.

---

32. Jim Dofka is a guitarist, songwriter, recording engineer and guitar teacher based in Pennsylvania. Learn more at www.jimdofka.com.

Mary told Matt Coe of *Dead Rhetoric* that one of the intents of *When Angels Kill* was to try and develop a younger power metal audience.

"We were trying to do something special and give people a reason to listen in an environment where you're basically in a snowstorm of things being released and vying for peoples' attention," Mary said of the lyrical concept of *When Angels Kill*. "I'm super proud of the record."

Despite its grandiose design, not everyone in the band was on board with the storyline at first.

"We actually had a framework of a story that we had worked on and sent around to the whole band, and everybody looked at it," Mary said. "A funny story, I remember our bass player, John, he got the story, and he goes, 'Do you have any other ideas? … He wasn't necessarily a big fan of the story. … We just started making the record, and he heard some of the songs, and he's like, 'Wow,' and he was very excited about it. So, the more material we started doing, and the more the songs started coming together, he just heard it, and he was excited like we were. I think we were all feeling something really special was happening. Musically, we were happy with it. And I think, I always say this in interviews, but if we're happy with it, and we're feeling excited about it, then we kind of know we're on to something."

Released on June 16, 2023, via Nuclear Blast, *When Angels Kill* featured three singles: the title track, "We Are Immortal," and "Resist the Tyrant." All three songs received a full music video treatment. The videos were directed by Lance Gergar. The videos feature a stand-in guitar player for Brosh—Brent Barker.[33] The record was produced by Mary, and recorded and engineered by Mary, Macko, Archer and Steve Conley. Mary and Conley mixed the album, and *When Angels Kill* was mastered by Lasse Lammert. Marta Gabriel provided background vocals, and the character voice over work was recorded by Scott Tunnix, Olivia Warren, Peter Baker, and Scott Jeffers.

The album's cover art was handled by Andy Pilkington, who also illustrated the last several Flotsam and Jetsam album covers. The front cover of *When Angels Kill* features a female angel with red hair, sporting a burning angel wing on one side, and a divine, white wing on the other side. The angel is depicted walking through an urban wasteland. In addition, Fifth Angel's logo was updated, with the band's name appearing with sharp edges and blades.

"Andy, he is kind of a genius. I sent some information on the songs, some of the lyrics, and this was the first thing he came back with," Mary said of the cover art. "The label and the band thought it was perfect for a number of reasons. There's almost a dual meaning going on with that cover. You have an angel where half the angel is good and half the angel is bad, everybody thinks of angels as guardians, and they are protecting me. On this album it's about when angels come here to bring destruction."

Reactions to *When Angels Kill* were mostly positive. JP from *Metal-Rules.com* gave it a stellar 4.5/5 rating, calling the production "modern and heavy" and the band's "heaviest

---

33. Barker has performed with members of Whitesnake, Foreigner, Montrose, and Kingdom Come. The guitarist also appears on a variety of recordings, including his own solo material. Check out his work at www.brentbarkermusic.com.

and fastest" record to-date. Similarly, *My Global Mind* ranked *When Angels Kill* a 9/10, calling the record "world class power/heavy metal" and "a monumental release."

On the flip side, while *Sputnik Music* judged *When Angels Kill* as "excellent," their review noted that the record's almost 70-minute runtime was a detracting factor. "Seventy minutes of anything gets exhausting and the album's bloat gets to be hard to ignore after a while," reviewer "PsychicChris" wrote. "While none of the songs are outright bad, the mounting time can make them trickier to sort out." A few reviews also called attention to the similarity between Flotsam and Jetsam's recent material, and what was on Fifth Angel's *When Angels Kill*. (Not surprising, given the involvement of Mary and Conley in both bands.)

Fifth Angel's *When Angels Kill* charted for one week in Germany, peaking at #50. It also made the top 100 music chart in Switzerland, clocking in at #74 for one week. The band returned to Germany for the Keep it True festival again on April 21, 2023. Fifth Angel performed two of their new songs, "When Angels Kill" and "We Are Immortal" in the 16-song set, whetting the appetites of fans for the group's new album, which would be released two months later. The show also featured two individual spotlights: a guitar solo by Brosh and a drum solo by Mary.

It took over a full year after the release of *When Angels Kill* for Fifth Angel to properly support the album. And to the delight of fans in Europe, they did it by doing the band's first-ever tour.

A full-on tour was not what Fifth Angel originally had in mind to support *When Angels Kill*. The band initially wanted to continue playing the festival circuit and expanding to events they had not previously appeared at. But Fifth Angel was having difficulty getting those bookings in Europe. Archer started researching promoters but realized that he did not have the right connections to make any inroads. But the guitarist knew someone who did—Jeffrey McCormack.

Archer and McCormack had kept in close contact since 2017, and Archer turned to his friend and former drummer to see if McCormack could "grease the wheels" a bit and help get Fifth Angel connected with the right people in the industry. McCormack was happy to help, but once he started looking into things, he quickly realized Fifth Angel had shot themselves in the foot.

McCormack explained that John Macko tried to be proactive and book a bunch of festival appearances for the band. But a few of the members had conflicts, so Fifth Angel had to back out.

"They did that with a very popular booking agent in Europe, Dragon Productions," McCormack said. "Once Fifth Angel canceled those festivals, it burned them. Ed asked me to call some agents, and I started calling around and everybody I was calling was like, 'No, we're not interested.'"

McCormack told Archer that Fifth Angel's previous cancelations left a bad taste in booking agents' mouths, and because the band had not played many shows, they did not have statistics to show promoters they could be a good draw for festivals. But instead of throwing in the towel, McCormack had another idea. Putting Fifth Angel on an old school club tour, where they could show the band was reliable, and build some positive numbers through a grassroots effort. Archer took the idea to his bandmates, and while there was some initial hesitation, they agreed to let McCormack book a tour for them.

Jeffrey went to work, booking Fifth Angel at two small, related festivals, the Storm Crusher Festival in Germany, and Pyrenean Warriors Open Air VIII in France.[34] McCormack was able to negotiate enough money from those appearances so that the band could finance traveling through Europe. With the festival shows booked, McCormack was asked by Fifth Angel to book as many gigs as he could for them in a two-week period, to consider it a real tour. McCormack was able to get Fifth Angel approximately €1,000 per show, plus their accommodations and travel. The band accepted it, and Fifth Angel's first-ever tour was finally announced.

McCormack was not the only one scheduling things for Fifth Angel, however. While McCormack booked the shows, Macko spent months making the travel arrangements for the band, which in Europe consisted of driving vans across several countries and flying to others. Macko also served as Fifth Angel's tour manager on the trek.

Prior to leaving the United States, however, Fifth Angel made an appearance at ProgPower USA XXIII, the annual festival held at Center Stage, in Atlanta, Georgia. Fifth Angel's 12-song performance at ProgPower relied heavily on material from the band's first album, but the group also debuted "Resist the Tyrant" from *When Angels Kill*. The show was a launching pad for Fifth Angel's tour, but there was one hitch—Ken Mary would not be accompanying his bandmates across the Atlantic.

The drummer was having some health issues at the time that could have been exacerbated by being on tour. So, after

---

34. Ironically, Fifth Angel had to cancel its appearance at Pyrenean Warriors Open Air. This was due to logistical issues trying to make the other shows on the band's tour.

playing ProgPower, Mary ceded his drum throne temporarily to Marco Prij, who plays in the bands Aphelion and Cryptosis, and works as a session drummer. Prij has a history of stepping in for bands when needed, and Mary was appreciative of and grateful for Prij filling in for him.[35] Prij rehearsed with Fifth Angel once when they arrived in Europe, and then it was off to the races.

"He did a really nice job and saved the tour," Mary said. "If it wasn't for him, we would've lost a ton of money, because I wasn't able to get there, period."

"Marco did a really good job, especially for a half a day of practice," added Macko. "He was pretty freaking good."

Fifth Angel's first tour went extremely well. With Brosh capable of singing harmony and background vocals, it gave Macko the freedom to increase his stage presence. The bassist jumped at the opportunity to prowl around the stage, and Carlson loved every minute of it.

"John came alive, running around, headbanging, he went nuts," Carlson said. "He wasn't strapped to the microphone, and it was great to really see him just really have fun."

As with any tour, some shows were attended better than others. Macko admitted that Fifth Angel's history of cancelations had many of the club owners concerned, but that apprehension ended up being unwarranted. Fifth Angel showed up, played spectacularly, and drew well. Fans from two or three countries away in Europe traveled extensively to see Fifth Angel perform. It resulted in a lot of energy at the shows, which the band truly appreciated.

"On the European tour, when we would go to a different

---

35. Prij also stepped in for Ken Mary when the latter needed to miss some Flotsam and Jetsam shows.

city, we would see somebody who came to the show the night before just going back home," Brosh said. "People kept coming up to us saying, 'We have been waiting to see you play live since the first album.' The appreciation that some of the people had there was just unreal. All the shows were good. Some of them were bigger, some of them were smaller, but we would finish playing a song and the lights would turn off, and the whole crowd would be chanting, 'Fifth Angel, Fifth Angel!' It was amazing."

Once Fifth Angel returned stateside from the *When Angels Kill* tour, the band was excited to continue playing live. They asked McCormack to reach out to some of the booking agents for U.S. rock and metal festivals. While McCormack was able to secure a spot at the Hell's Heroes Festival for Fifth Angel in 2025, getting additional gigs has been a bit of a challenge, again, due to the band's history of canceling appearances.

Fifth Angel scrubbed two appearances at Legions of Metal Fest in Chicago during recent years, which has now backfired on the band. McCormack has done his best to change the negative perception some booking agents have about Fifth Angel, but it has been an uphill climb. In addition, Fifth Angel's former drummer was helping the band for free, so when things didn't work out, and McCormack was criticized internally, it left a sour taste in his mouth.

"It was not a very pleasurable experience for me," McCormack said. "There was a lot of tug-of-war on what the band wanted to do, where they wanted to go, how much time they wanted to spend and all this stuff. Initially, I was just a pal helping them out, and really helping Ed out mostly, but I love the other guys too. I wanted to help, but will I do it beyond this? No."

As of June 2025, Fifth Angel's prospects for the future are unclear. While the band is interested in playing more shows, Macko said he felt it was only worth it if Fifth Angel can get to a higher financial level in a relatively short period of time. The bassist is not interested in doing another tour unless they have the funding to hire a dedicated tour manager and a crew to take care of things.

From a monetary standpoint, Fifth Angel's 2024 European tour was deemed successful. The band turned a profit and the fan turnout to the see shows was above expectations. But managing the tour was too stressful for Macko and the rest of the band to do consistently on their own.

"I was the babysitter, the mother hen, I collected the money, I'm the one that counted the merchandise sales," Macko said. "I'm the one that had to yell at everybody to be down at the van by 10:30 a.m. and all that crap. It took a toll on me, and I got very sick after the tour. I won't ever do that again."

That statement aside, Macko maintained that Fifth Angel loves to perform, and wants to play gigs. But the finances and infrastructure need to be in place so that it makes sense for the band. For the time being, that means Fifth Angel will focus primarily on playing festivals, with a few one-off performances.

From Brosh's perspective, the guitarist said he is younger than his bandmates and probably a bit more flexible in terms of the schedule. Brosh remains enthusiastic about bringing Fifth Angel's music to the masses. Whether it is a long club tour or just playing as many festival dates as possible, Brosh would like to get on the road. But he said Fifth Angel's decision-making is a bit unique from what he has seen with other bands, which complicates things.

"You're looking at a drummer, bass player, and guitar player making the decisions for a band," Brosh said, referring to Mary, Macko, and Archer, respectively. "It's a very strange dynamic, and they also don't see eye to eye on a lot of things, and it becomes a situation where there's too many cooks in the kitchen. Between them, somebody's going to just not want to play a show or something. Unfortunately, things are not moving along as much as I would have liked to have seen. I would love for Fifth Angel to be a lot more active."

One thing is for certain—the fans want to see Fifth Angel more frequently. For example, before Fifth Angel played the Hell's Heroes festival on Thursday, March 20, 2025, in Houston, Texas, Lillian Axe drummer Wayne Stokley took to social media and wrote that he has "been waiting my whole life to enter the cathedral" and see the band live. In the same thread, fan Andy L. responded that he saw Fifth Angel play the ProgPower festival on September 6, 2024, in Atlanta, Georgia, and that they "were incredible."

When and if Fifth Angel resumes playing live, Archer said he'd like to see the band incorporate more of the material from *The Third Secret* into its repertoire on a regular basis. He noted both "Dust to Dust" and "Stars Are Falling" are fun to play and fit in Fifth Angel's set well. But he admitted the band would have to play a longer set time to likely do so, which might not be feasible if Fifth Angel only plays festival dates.

Whether Fifth Angel records new music is also up in the air. Archer has said he would like to do one final Fifth Angel record where he is more involved in the writing and creative process. The guitarist was mostly absent from the songwriting sessions for *The Third Secret* and *When Angels*

Kill. But Mary wasn't sure the band had another album in them. The drummer called *When Angels Kill* a "labor of love" that the band members all feel upholds the legacy of the Fifth Angel name. But by using the lyrics and themes of past Fifth Angel records to construct the story behind *When Angels Kill*, Mary questioned where the group could go lyrically.

"I'm never going to say never, but if we ever do another Fifth Angel album, maybe we should change direction a bit lyrically," Mary said. "Not necessarily musically different, but I think for everybody to get on board and do another one, we're going to have to have some real reason to make that happen."

Oliver Weinsheimer chimed in on the possibility of new Fifth Angel music as well, praising the talents of vocalist Steve Carlson. Weinsheimer called Carlson "the best thing to happen" to Fifth Angel and would like to see how the band evolves with him.

"I wish they would make a new album, but more in the style of the first two with a more warm and natural sound," Weinsheimer added. "I am sure they still have it in their blood to do that."

Time will tell how Fifth Angel's future unfolds. But given how unorthodox the band's journey has been so far, it likely won't go according to plan. Regardless, Fifth Angel's impact on listeners over the last 40 years is undeniable. The band's followers are still eager to see them perform, and Fifth Angel's "cult status" amongst heavy metal fans remains firm.

"This music is timeless, plus it has a big budget songwriting quality to it," Weinsheimer added. "People grew up with it and [because] the band never played live back then, they have a certain mystery around themselves.

This is why the first shows went down so amazingly. People were hot for it. They had a certain underdog status and people respect that."

Describing the connection between Fifth Angel and the band's fans is difficult. But perhaps Ted Pilot said it best in the lyrics he wrote over 40 years ago: "You know it's a feeling. Like a memory from a spark. It all came together when Fifth Angel left his mark."

When Angels Kill is a concept album that weaves the lyrical themes from Fifth Angel's first three records into a story.

Promotional poster for Fifth Angel's European Tour in 2024.
Image courtesy of Fifth Angel.

Ken Mary and Ed Archer in April 2024. The two have been friends for nearly 50 years. Photo courtesy of Fifth Angel.

Steven Carlson performs at the Keep it True Festival, in Lauda-Königshofen, Germany, on April 21, 2023. Photo by and courtesy of Michael "Paranoid" Hoenninger.

Ethan Brosh shredding at the Keep it True Festival, in Lauda-Königshofen, Germany, on April 21, 2023. Photo by and courtesy of Michael "Paranoid" Hoenninger.

Ed Archer, John Macko, and Steven Carlson performing at the Keep it True Festival, in Lauda-Königshofen, Germany, on April 21, 2023. Photo by and courtesy of Michael "Paranoid" Hoenninger.

Fifth Angel rocking the crowd at the Keep it True Festival, in Lauda-Königshofen, Germany, on April 21, 2023. Photo by and courtesy of Michael "Paranoid" Hoenninger.

Epilogue

Fifth Angel's self-titled debut album struck a chord with thousands of metalheads in 1986, propelling the band to cult status. To this day, media outlets consistently rank *Fifth Angel* as one of the top metal albums of the 1980s. For example, Chris Jennings, writing for *Worship Metal* in 2020, ranked *Fifth Angel* #24 in a list of the best 30 heavy metal albums of 1986.

"Fifth Angel were simply a heavy metal band in the purist terms; having more in common with the likes of Dio than the prevailing trends of the year," Jennings wrote. "[T]he hard-hitting anthemic likes of 'In the Fallout' and "Call Out the Warning" distances them from the glam-metal shenanigans of Poison, Cinderella and Warrant, etc."

The people responsible for Fifth Angel's first recording are all, as of this writing, alive and well. Only Ed Archer and Ken Mary remain active with the band, but the group still performs sporadic shows as opportunities arise.

Archer got married in the 1990s and had a son with his then wife. The couple eventually split up in the late-2000s. The guitarist has since remarried and now has a stepdaughter. When not crafting song demos or performing with Fifth Angel, Ed works in the electronics field.

Ken Mary has been married to his longtime love, Leslie, for many years. The drummer is one of the busiest musicians in the world, playing for both Fifth Angel and Flotsam and Jetsam. Ken continues to operate his studio, SonicPhish Productions, and he appears on a variety of musical projects as time permits.

As for the rest of the original quartet, James Byrd is doing well, living a healthy life in rural Washington. The guitar wizard has put down his six-string axes in favor of another passion—dirt bike riding. He is happy and content with his peaceful life.

Ted Pilot retired from his career as an endodontist and now serves as CEO of a manufacturing company. Pilot's career change opened his schedule enough to where he would like to get involved with music again. Unfortunately, chronic nasal issues that doctors are not able to correct now prevent Pilot from singing for more than a few minutes at a time. Ted's condition has effectively ended his singing career and is the primary reason he was not able to rejoin Fifth Angel.

"Performing in front of people, singing, was the highlight of my life, I would say," Pilot said. "To not be able to do that, it's unfortunate, but don't feel sorry for me. I just had to take a different road. Music brings people together and it's an awesome thing that I've been able to participate in, and I'll never regret it. I just wish I could have done more of it."

Regarding the remaining "classic" members of Fifth Angel, after a long career in the information technology field, John Macko is retired and enjoying life in Florida. He got married again in 2024, continues to write new music, and provides the bass groove for Fifth Angel whenever called upon.

Kendall Bechtel remains somewhat of an enigma. He continues to write and record his own music and perform cover tunes as a tribute to his musical influences.[36] But unfortunately, repeated attempts to contact him for this book went unanswered. At the time of this writing in

---

36. Check out Kendall Bechtel's official YouTube channel at https://www.youtube.com/@kendallbechtel759.

2025, many of Bechtel's former Fifth Angel bandmates had not heard from the guitarist in a couple of years. It is this author's hope that Kendall is enjoying life and is happy and proud of his work with Fifth Angel. Thank you, Kendall, for some great music and memories.

Acknowledgements

The roots of *Wings of Destiny: The Story of Fifth Angel* run deep, spanning over a quarter-century, back to my very first email exchange with James Byrd. When I first dropped him a line in the late-1990s, Byrd noted the "444" in my email address, which started a long conversation about the possible meanings of that number. (Byrd has a song called "Metatron 444" on his *Crimes of Virtuosity* album.) While I am not one who subscribes deeply to beliefs about numbers, that first interaction with Byrd was a major factor that helped us reconnect when I started this book.

When I was conducting interviews with Fifth Angel band members, I reached out to Byrd after not having talked to him in almost 20 years. My signature number of "444" again got his attention. Eventually, he felt comfortable enough to provide further perspective on Fifth Angel's early history for posterity. Thank you for trusting me to express your thoughts, James. I am very glad you are at peace and enjoying life.

My connection with Ed Archer was just as vital for this book to come to life. Ed and I have been good friends since 2007, sharing with each other much of the ups and downs we've experienced as our lives unfolded. If you've read this far, I'm sure you remember my story of visiting Ed's home for Fifth Angel's 2010 rehearsal. It was there where I first thought about writing the band's biography.

Over the ensuing years, I told Ed that I would chronicle Fifth Angel's legacy in a book. At first, Ed didn't think there was enough of a story to tell. But I assured him that there was, and I would eventually fulfill my promise.

Fast-forward to 2024, when I first started writing in earnest, Ed was the first person other than my wife who knew this biography on Fifth Angel was happening. Ed spent many hours on the phone with me over the span of five months, providing intricate details about the formation of Fifth Angel, and all the issues the band worked through over the years. When I asked him to write the book's foreword, Ed never hesitated, saying he was honored to do it. After that, when all the writing was done, Ed then graciously sent photographs and scans of historic band documents to me, so they could appear in this book.

Simply put, *Wings of Destiny: The Story of Fifth Angel* would not have happened without the involvement and support of Ed Archer. Thank you, my friend, for always being there for me.

Speaking of support, writing a book is an emotional roller coaster. My wife Staci and our daughter Samantha were rocks for me throughout this entire project. They encouraged me when things got tough and graciously understood when I needed to miss dinner or reschedule some family events so I could meet deadlines and get writing done. They kept me going, particularly when things went sideways near the end. I love you both, and thank you for always having my back.

In addition, it should come as no surprise that publishing a book takes a village. My heartfelt thanks to the following individuals for being there (either in real time or in spirit) when I needed you: The late Debbie and Richard Heaton, my brother Todd Heaton and his family, Gregory Twachtman, the late Jason Slater, Cyrus Wraith Walker, Brett Miller, Brian Naron, James Beach, Scott Thompson, Richie Waddell, Jonathan Rustvold, Jeff Brown, Jeffrey Douglass, Wayne Douglass, the late Robert Kotynski, Derek Simon, Bobby Ferkovich, Marty Temme, Michael "Paranoid" Hoenninger, Mike Gaube, Jeff Wagner, Alex Ward, and Kory Pohlman.

And last, but certainly not least, my heartfelt thanks to all the members of Fifth Angel, past and present. Your music was, and continues to be, an inspiration. My best wishes to all of you, and your families.

Author Interviews

Ed Archer (Sein)
Tim Branom
Ethan Brosh
James Byrd
Steve Carlson
Mike Gaube
John Luke Hébert
Kenny Kay
John Macko
Ken K. Mary
Jeffrey McCormack
Peter Orullian
Ted Pilot
Derek Simon
Richard Stuverud
Oliver Weinsheimer

Works Cited

James R. Beach, et al., *Rusted Metal* (1st ed. 2019) NW Metalworx Books.

James D. Sutton, "Ed Archer Interview (Fifth Angel/Glass/Ridge)" *Rusted Metal* (1st ed. 2019) NW Metalworx Books.

Brett Van Putt, "Interview with Guitarist James Byrd" (Dec. 2002) *tMetal.com*.

Rick Maloney, "Interview with James Byrd" (Sep. 2002) *MetalRules.com*.

Interview with James Byrd, (Aug. 2002) *Heavy Metal Resource*.

Interview with James Byrd, (2000) *Rock Reunion*.

Brian J. Heaton, "A Fade to Flames" (interview with John Macko and Kendall Bechtel) *FifthAngel.net* (Sep. 2006).

Brian J. Heaton, "Ted Pilot Explains Fifth Angel's Demise and Aborted Reunion" *FifthAngel.net* (2007).

Joe Lalaina, "Fifth Angel – Heaven Sent" (Feb. 1989) *RIP*.

Dave Reynolds, "More Northwest Metal" (1987) *Metal Forces*.

Edgar Klüsener, "The Fifth Dimension" (1989) *Metal Hammer*.

Laurel Fishman, "Fifth Angel: Fifth Angel" (album review) (1988) *RIP*.

Dawn Anderson, "Rising Out of the Eastside" (May 10, 1988) *Journal-American*.

Jon Hotten, "5th Angels" (Feb. 1988) *Kerrang!*

Malcolm Dome, "Angelic Upstarts" (Nov. 1986) *Kerrang!*

Adrianne Stone, "Fifth Angel: Pacific Coast Powerhouses Unleash Debut Disc".

Joe Anthony, "Interview with Ted Pilot and John Macko" (1988) *KISS FM*.

John Kindred, "Interview with James Byrd" (July 2011) *Hardrock Haven*.

Kevin Tanza, "Fifth Angel – The Making and History of Their Debut Album" (Aug. 12, 2021) *MusikHolics*.

Dave Ling, "Fifth Angel: Send Me An Angel" (1988) *Metal Hammer*.

Pavlos Giannakopoulos, "Interview with Jeffrey McCormack" *Rock Overdose*.

Chris Hawkins, "Album Review: Fifth Angel – The Third Secret" (Oct. 19, 2018) *Antihero*.

Mark Diggins, "Album Review: Fifth Angel – The Third Secret" (Oct. 27, 2018) *The Rockpit*.

Rodrigo Altaf, "Fifth Angel – The Third Secret (Album Review) (Oct. 5, 2018) *Sonic Perspectives*.

Chris Jennings, "The 30 Greatest Metal Albums of 1986!" (Mar. 29, 2020) *Worship Metal*.

JP, "Fifth Angel-When Angels Kill" (Aug. 1, 2023) *Metal-Rules.com*.

Smudge, "Fifth Angel – When Angels Kill Review" (Jun. 27, 2023) *My Global Mind*.

Janiss Garza, "Fifth Angel: All in Good Time" (1989).

Andrea Long and Michele Klossner, "Interview with Ted Pilot and Kendall Bechtel" (Dec. 1989) *City Heat*.

Mike Gaube, "Interview with Fifth Angel" (2018).

Cathy Rankin, "Interview with Fifth Angel" (2023).

Matt Coe, "Fifth Angel – Older, Wiser, and Ready to Kill" (Jul. 16, 2023) *Dead Rhetoric*.

Fifth Angel Concert History

- April 24, 2010 - Lauda-Königshofen, Germany – Tauberfrankenhalle – Keep It True XIII
  - Note: Fifth Angel's first official show.

- April 22, 2017 – Seattle, Washington, USA – El Corazón
  - Note: Fifth Angel's first official show in Seattle and the United States. Headline appearance.

- April 29, 2017 - Lauda-Königshofen, Germany – Tauberfrankenhalle – Keep It True XX

- February 16, 2019 - Würzburg, Germany – Posthalle – Metal Assault Festival 2019

- June 9, 2019 – Gelsenkirchen, Germany – Amphitheater Gelsenkirchen – Rock Hard Festival 2019

- August 10, 2019 – Kortrijk, Belgium – Sport Campus Lange Munte – Alcatraz Metal Festival 2019

- April 21, 2023 - Lauda-Königshofen, Germany – Tauberfrankenhalle – Keep It True XXIII

- September 6, 2024 – Atlanta, Georgia – Center Stage – ProgPower USA XXIII
  - Note: Fifth Angel's first show in the United States outside of Seattle.

- September 10, 2024 – Mannheim, Germany – 7er Club
    - Note: Fifth Angel's first non-festival show outside of the U.S.
- September 11, 2024 – Trübbach, Switzerland – Jonnys Lion-Cave
- September 13, 2024 - Püchersreuth, Germany – O'Schnitt Halle Wurz (Storm Crusher Festival)
- ~~September 14, 2024 – Torreilles, France - Site De Juhègues (Pyrenean Warriors Open Air VIII)~~ (This appearance was booked and promoted, but Fifth Angel canceled due to logistical issues.)
- September 16, 2024 – Zagreb, Croatia – Hard Place
- September 17, 2024 – Belgrade, Serbia – Klub Fest – Zemun
- September 19, 2024 – Hamburg, Germany – Bambi Galore
- September 21, 2024 – Athens, Greece – Kyttaro
- September 22, 2024 – Thessaloniki, Greece – Eightball Club
- March 20, 2025 – Houston, Texas – The Lawn at White Oak (Hell's Heroes festival)

Author Bio

BRIAN J. HEATON is the author of *Jason Slater: For the Sake of Supposing* and *Roads to Madness: The Touring History of Queensrÿche (1981-1997)*. He also co-wrote *Building an Empire: The Story of Queensrÿche*, the first biography on the band.

Brian got his start as a professional writer in 1998, reporting on the military sports and fitness industry for two trade magazines. After earning his Juris Doctor in 2003, Brian entered the political communications realm for a decade, before returning to journalism in the 2010s. He spent several years as a senior writer covering public sector technology, law, and policy for various news outlets.

A proud native of Long Island, New York, Brian now resides in Northern California with his family.

www.ingramcontent.com/pod-product-compliance
Lightning Source LLC
Chambersburg PA
CBHW071737150426
43191CB00010B/1607